Slaying Leviathan

SLAYING
LEVIATHAN

LIMITED GOVERNMENT AND RESISTANCE
IN THE CHRISTIAN TRADITION

GLENN S.
SUNSHINE

canonpress
Moscow, Idaho

Published by Canon Press
P. O. Box 8729, Moscow, Idaho 83843
800-488-2034 | www.canonpress.com

Cover design by James Engerbretson
Interior design by Valerie Anne Bost
Printed in the United States of America

Unless otherwise indicated, all Scripture quotations are from the King James Version. All Bible quotations marked ESV are from the English Standard Version copyright ©2001 by Crossway Bibles, a division of Good News Publishers. Used by permission.

Library of Congress Cataloguing-in-Publication data:
Sunshine, Glenn S., 1958- author.
Slaying Leviathan : limited government and resistance in the
   Christian tradition / Glenn S. Sunshine.
Moscow, Idaho : Canon Press, [2021]
LCCN 2020049298 | ISBN 9781952410727 (paperback)
LCSH: Christianity and politics. | Church and state. |
   Liberty—Religious aspects—Christianity. | Christianity and
   politics—United States. | Church and state—United States.
Classification: LCC BR115.P7 S86 2021 | DDC 261.7—dc23
LC record available at https://lccn.loc.gov/2020049298

21 22 23 24 25   10 9 8 7 6 5 4 3

CONTENTS

Introduction 1

1 The Early Church 7

2 Augustine 19

3 Church, State & the Limits of Power 35

4 Natural Rights in the Middle Ages 53

5 Law & Government in the Protestant Reformation 69

6 Protestant Resistance Theory 95

7 Resistance Theory in Britain 113

8 Locke in Context 129

9 The American Founders 149

   Epilogue 169

   Suggestions for Further Reading 179

   Acknowledgments 181

DEDICATION

To C.R. Wiley and Tom Price,
my partners in crime at the *Theology Pugcast*

INTRODUCTION

The condition upon which God hath given liberty to man is eternal vigilance; which condition if he break, servitude is at once the consequence of his crime and the punishment of his guilt.

—JOHN PHILPOT CURRAN (1750–1817)

In 1789, a revolution broke out in France. Rejecting the past, especially Christianity, the revolutionaries built their program on autonomous human reason and Enlightenment ideals, with the result that in the name of liberty, equality, and brotherhood, the leaders of the revolution slaughtered over one hundred thousand of their own people.

What went wrong?

No matter how much the revolutionary government trumpeted its support of liberty, like any good propagandists, they redefined the term. Following Rousseau, they claimed that true freedom was found in submitting to the "general will," which of course they alone understood and embodied. And if you did not agree, if you insisted on your own faith or defended your right to property or were found wanting in revolutionary fervor, your existence threatened the promised utopia, and you had to be eliminated.

This is what happens in crisis situations when the government claims the right to control all areas of life. You end up with a totalitarian nightmare, a monster that reaches into everything we do, everything we say, everything we think, that claims authority over everything we own and lets us live only in line with its values and interests.

What you get is Leviathan.

We are able to put a name to this monstrous form of government thanks to Thomas Hobbes. In 1651, he published a book on political theory called *Leviathan* in which he argued that the king had absolute authority in the kingdom. This meant that, by definition, a king could not violate laws or deprive people of their rights because all authority had been ceded to him by the people.

Although Hobbes had some unique arguments in the book, his basic idea was not new. The spirit of Leviathan had shaped many cultures in the ancient world, most notably the Roman Empire. "Caesar is Lord," the de facto creed of the Empire, implied that Caesar had supreme authority over civic life because he was the embodiment of the state. Nothing was beyond Leviathan's grasp. This included religion: to pledge allegiance to the state, a Roman burned incense to the statue of the emperor as an act of worship. Even when there was a dispute within temples and priesthoods, the emperor intervened as mediator to resolve it.

This was not the world as God created it to be governed. In Eden, Adam and Eve were free to enjoy the beauty of the Garden, to develop its resources under God's authority, to act with creativity and liberty, and to enjoy the fruits of their labors. Sin ruined all of this, and from the time of Babel through the present, governments have sought unlimited power over the bodies, minds, and hearts of their subjects.

Jesus was born into such a world. In the first century and afterward, the Christian confession "Jesus is Lord" (e.g., Rom. 10:9) was a direct challenge to Caesar's authority. As worshippers of one God, Christians could not participate in burning incense to the emperor or treating him in any sense as divine. The result was centuries of sporadic persecution for the church. But something remarkable happened: even though Christians were an unpopular, persecuted minority, Christianity continued to spread such that in AD 313, the Roman Emperor Constantine issued the Edict of Milan, declaring religious liberty in the Empire and thus decriminalizing Christianity.

The church had existed for three hundred years without state support—surviving and thriving even with the murderous opposition of the Caesars. In the end, this dealt Leviathan a mortal wound, demonstrating that the church was separate from and independent of the state. A king's reach was limited, extending only to the things that were Caesar's, not to the church or to the things that were God's.

But what, precisely, does belong to Caesar?

To answer this question, Christian thinkers throughout the millennia have focused on a wide range of issues, most of which were intended to address specific legal, political, or religious questions current at the particular time each was writing. *Slaying Leviathan* surveys some of the key elements of Christian political thought, specifically those that were ultimately synthesized into a coherent political philosophy by John Locke, who was himself arguing against the spirit of Leviathan in his day. Locke is rightly viewed as an Enlightenment thinker, but the central elements of his political philosophy were adapted from the Christian tradition. And Locke of course influenced the American Founders, who represent the culmination of the Christian political philosophy surveyed in this book.

The American Founders intended to put an end to Leviathan by adopting a system based on principles of unalienable rights and limited government. But unfortunately, like the Beast rising from the sea in the Apocalypse, Leviathan's mortal wound has healed (Rev. 13:3). Through the decisions of the philosopher-kings of the U.S. Supreme Court, the abdication of legislative responsibilities by Congress to the Executive Branch, and the expansion of the regulatory state, the reach of government has never been larger in American history than it is now. Leviathan's tentacles have wriggled their way into all areas of life, even regulating the conditions under which churches can meet and what they can do in worship.

The government we have now would have been unrecognizable to the Founders, and our acquiescence to its systematic encroachments on liberty would have infuriated them.

But here is the point: it would not surprise them. They were well acquainted with the tendency of governments to turn tyrannical. A popular quote in the nineteenth century frequently attributed to Jefferson says, "Eternal vigilance is the price we pay for liberty." If we are to maintain our liberty, we must constantly be on guard against the rise of Leviathan. We must play Whac-A-Mole with it whenever it rears its head.

Our cultural complacency in this area has allowed Leviathan to be reborn, leading to the politicization of every area of society as everything becomes subject to the regulatory state.

As a church historian, I decided I needed to address this problem because of the actions of an administration that worked to undermine religious liberty, and with it a host of other liberties. I began studying the development of Christian political theology, and I discovered there the sources of our ideas about limited government, unalienable rights, liberty, and resistance to tyranny as well as resources to help us think through how we are to respond to today's challenges. Examining the long Christian tradition of resisting the totalizing tendencies of government proves to be very relevant to us in view of the deterioration of our liberty. Revisiting our Christian tradition is also the first step we must take as we consider what to do about Leviathan rising.

In each of the following chapters, I summarize the development of a different aspect of the Christian political tradition that contributed to the thinking of the American Founders and discuss some of the implications of those

ideas for today. Through it all, you will learn the story of
Christianity's battle against Leviathan, a battle waged in
the name of the liberty God granted all humanity in the
Garden of Eden.

CHAPTER 1
THE EARLY CHURCH

If you wish to defend religion by bloodshed, and by tortures, and by guilt, it will no longer be defended, but will be polluted and profaned. For nothing is so much a matter of free-will as religion; in which, if the mind of the worshiper is disinclined to it, religion is at once taken away and ceases to exist. —LACTANTIUS (250-320)

THE FIRST 300 YEARS

From its earliest days, Christianity has had a complex relationship with the state. Jesus was clear that His kingdom is not of this world (John 18:36) and, therefore, that His work was not about political power. He also taught that we are to give to Caesar (i.e., the government) the things that are Caesar's, which means that Caesar really does have legitimate claims on us (Matt. 22:21; Mark 12:17; Luke 20:25). At the same time, however, that claim is not all-encompassing: we are to give to God, not to Caesar, the things that belong to God. The government may not take on authority that properly belongs to God or, by extension, to the church. What things are properly outside the scope of government became the subject of much political and theological reflection over the centuries.

In its most basic form, the question of what properly belonged to God and not to Caesar arose within a few decades of Jesus's death and resurrection. As touched on in the introduction, one of the earliest Christian confessions was "Jesus is Lord." Most people today do not understand how significant and radical that statement was in the context of the Roman Empire. The de facto imperial confession was "Caesar is Lord," that is, Caesar is sovereign in this world and has authority over just about every aspect of life. The title *Lord* even implied a kind of divinity for Caesar. Confessing "Jesus is Lord" (implying that Caesar is not) therefore had unmistakable political overtones that could not help but sound treasonous to Roman ears.

The status of the Christian confession was further complicated by another aspect of Roman culture. In Rome, deities were the supreme authorities in particular spheres of life or of the world. Thus, for example, Neptune was sovereign over the seas, and when you went out on them, you needed to acknowledge Neptune's authority by performing a sacrifice to him. Otherwise, you were risking his wrath. In the political world, the supreme authority was the emperor. This meant that he was periodically viewed as a god, and in all cases, his authority was recognized by performing some form of religious ritual such as burning incense to his statue. Jews had special rights that exempted them from this, but Christians did not, particularly when the church was increasingly made up of Gentile converts.

For Romans, burning incense to the statue of the emperor had little more significance than saying the Pledge of Allegiance today. But to Christians, it was idolatry, giving to Caesar the things that are God's. So although they did their best to live quiet and peaceable lives following Paul's exhortation (1 Tim. 2:2), they adamantly refused to participate in worship of pagan gods or of the emperor.

To put this in different terms, Jesus's own teaching led the church to the idea that government has its place but that its authority is limited. Combined with the confession of Jesus's lordship, this was a recipe for persecution in the power-obsessed world of ancient Rome. Sporadic persecution began under Nero (r. AD 54–68) and continuing for centuries. For their disloyalty to the emperor, for their refusal to worship pagan gods (which made them atheists in the eyes of the Romans), for their intolerant and bigoted belief that Jesus is the only hope of salvation, for their willingness to accept women and slaves as equal members of their community and even as leaders, and for a range of other practices that distinguished believers from their neighbors, Christians were held in contempt by the people of Rome. They were slandered; their beliefs were caricatured; their property was confiscated; and they watched as their friends, spouses, and children were tortured to death for the amusement of cheering crowds before they were martyred themselves.

But because of their faithfulness, the church ended up spreading and outlasting the mighty Roman Empire itself. Tertullian's dictum, "The blood of the martyrs is the seed of the church," is true. As the Romans watched Christians go to gruesome, horrible deaths willingly and even singing hymns, they developed a grudging admiration for their courage and commitment and inevitably began to ask themselves why anyone would go through that when all they had to do was burn a pinch of incense to the emperor. Christian faithfulness stood in sharp contrast to the faith of most Romans, who recognized that they did not have anything they would be willing to die that way for. And so, people were increasingly attracted to the church by the faithfulness of the martyrs.

The persecution of the church would lay the foundation for one of the core principles of Christian political theology: the church is a distinct institution from the State. Unlike other cultures of the ancient world, including Old Testament Israel, religion and government in Christianity are separate institutions with different spheres of authority and with distinct responsibilities. Both are ordained by God for his purposes in the world and in the best case can cooperate and work together toward the common goal of producing a just and peaceful society, but this is neither necessary or inevitable. The church can perform its work even in the face of murderous hostility from the government, and thus the two cannot properly ever be united into a single entity. Until Christ returns, theocracy is off the table.

THE CHURCH IN THE CHRISTIAN ROMAN EMPIRE

The church's situation changed radically when the Emperor Constantine converted and issued the Edict of Milan in AD 313. Constantine had long exposure to Christianity and even as a pagan had looked on it favorably. For example, he appointed Lactantius, a Berber Christian convert, as his son's tutor in 309. Lactantius wrote a work entitled *The Divine Institutes* in which, like other early Christian writers, he made an argument for religious liberty on the grounds that worship of God was only acceptable if it was offered freely.

In 312, Constantine was fighting Maxentius, a rival for the title of emperor, and is reported to have seen a vision of a cross with the words "In this sign, conquer." He had his soldiers paint a cross on their shields, and then defeated Maxentius at the Battle of the Milvian Bridge. As a result, he converted to Christianity (though there is some dispute on whether his conversion was genuine), and the following year he issued the Edict of Milan. Using wording and reasoning taken from Lactantius's *Divine Institutes*, this Edict established religious liberty in Rome, effectively making Christianity legal and ending religious persecution.

People often argue that Constantine made Christianity the official religion of the empire, thereby undermining the distinction between church and state. This is a fundamental misunderstanding of both Constantine and the Edict of Milan. Although Constantine legalized Christianity, he did not make it Rome's state religion. (That would only occur later with the Edict of Thessalonica issued by Theodosius I in AD 380.) And even after Constantine's edict, pagans continued to be allowed to worship within the Empire. Far from making Christianity the state religion, what the Edict of Milan did was to legalize all religions, not just Christianity. Further, as we have seen, the church had grown and expanded without government recognition for nearly three centuries. In fact, Christianity is the *only* major world religion to begin and spread without government support. Constantine's actions would not and could not change the precedent that had been set that church and government are separate institutions, and that the church can exist and function even in the face of government opposition.

THE STATE AND CONFLICTS IN THE CHURCH

In the Roman Empire, when a conflict arose within a religion, the emperor was responsible to act as a mediator to resolve the conflict. Thus, when a dispute arose in the church over whether Jesus was God incarnate, as taught by Athanasius, or the first and highest created being, as taught by Arius, Constantine did what emperors were supposed to do: He called a church council to settle the issue. The council was held in the city of Nicaea, now in modern Turkey, in AD 325. Although Constantine attended the council, the decision was made by the bishops without his interference. In other words, he provided a forum to solve the problem without dictating what the solution should be.

Constantine had a very different response to the Donatists. These were Christians who believed that priests who had acted faithlessly under persecution were never legitimate priests to begin with, and thus that all the sacraments that they had ever performed were invalid. This meant, for example, that anyone who had been baptized by a priest who later apostatized had to be rebaptized. In a dispute that we will examine in more detail in chapter 2, a church council decided against the Donatist position, and in response, the Donatists rioted. Constantine cracked down on them violently—no ruler can tolerate rioting, because it quickly turns into rebellion,[1] so Constantine responded to them as he would to any other rioters.

Augustine of Hippo, whose theology has shaped Christianity in the west more than that of any other thinker, would later support Constantine's reaction and the suppression of Donatism by state power. Augustine used Jesus's words *cogite intrare* ("compel them to enter," Luke 14:23) to argue that the state had the right and responsibility to coerce heretics (though not pagans) to rejoin the church. While this followed the ancient pattern of the state overseeing religious practice, it was inconsistent with the broader perspective that the church exists independent of the state; further, it violated the principle of religious liberty promoted by Lactantius and other, earlier Christian writers. As we will see in the next chapter, Augustine articulated some critically important ideas that would shape political theology in powerful ways for many centuries, but in this respect, he departed from the Christian tradition and helped set up the long centuries of cooperation between church and state in the coercion and persecution of religious dissenters.

---

1. This is a lesson it would be well for modern governors and mayors to learn.

On the other hand, the interaction between church and state was a two-way street in which church leaders called out even emperors when they acted immorally. The classic example is Ambrose of Milan, Augustine's mentor, who forced Emperor Theodosius I to perform public penance for ordering the massacre of people in Thessalonica after the murder of one of his officials there. To put it differently, emperors may have gotten involved in issues in the church, but church leaders also called emperors and government officials to task for the conduct of political affairs. The dynamics of this relationship would continue to be played out in many ways over the centuries to today, when, for example, Catholic priests have excluded politicians from Holy Communion for their support of abortion.

IMPLICATIONS

If asked how the Christian should relate to the government, early believers would tell you that their first and primary loyalty must always be to King Jesus. They obey the laws of the state insofar as they do not conflict with the laws of their king, but they would rather die than be disloyal to their true sovereign and lord even by simply attending quasi-religious events and festivities that contradicted their faith. The state has legitimate, God-given authority, but not ahead of Christ or over a Christian's conscience.

This was a groundbreaking idea. Up to the Edict of Milan, governments were essentially totalitarian: they claimed authority over every area of life, even supervising religious belief and practice and determining which religions would be accepted and which not. The decriminalization of Christianity after centuries of persecution meant that there was at least one public institution—the church—that was not directly under the authority of the state.

This immediately leads to the question of how church and state are to relate to each other. Where does the authority of one end and the other begin? Much of the political history of the Western world is connected to the tug-of-war to determine the proper boundaries in the relationship between religion and civil government. Sometimes the state gets the upper hand, and sometimes the church, but the dynamic caused by the tension between the two is a major element in the history of Western political thought.

But the distinction between church and state carries another, more subtle implication. If the government's authority is limited with respect to the church, if the state does not rule over all of life, then there might be other spheres where the government also cannot legitimately trespass. The medieval world worked out the logic of this idea by developing a range of mediating institutions that stand between the individual and the state. These range from the natural institution of the family, which had been largely recognized by Rome, to guilds, confraternities and other charitable agencies, business consortia, schools, etc. These institutions are collectively known as civil society.

The theory behind civil society—that government is not and should not be all powerful, and that there are segments of society that should not be under direct government control—would eventually crystallize in the idea of sphere sovereignty. Sphere sovereignty holds that society consists of a number of autonomous spheres that should properly regulate their own affairs. These include government, religion, family, education, business, labor, and others. Government in particular has a specific set of responsibilities related to defense against "all enemies, foreign and domestic," the enforcement of laws, and seeing to it that the spheres neither overstep their bounds nor violate the law.

Although each of these spheres should govern its own affairs, sometimes on a wide scale they do not: family structure collapses, schools fail to teach effectively, businesses act unethically, labor organizations become corrupt. When this happens, the temptation is for another sphere, almost inevitably the government, to step in to fix the problem rather than to work to revitalize the failing sphere(s). Unfortunately, government is ill-equipped to solve these problems—its tools and its competence lie in its areas of responsibility, not in those of other spheres. As a result, its attempts to step in and regulate the workings of another sphere are likely to be clumsy at best and often will make the problem worse. It is not alarmist to say, more ominously, that whenever a government oversteps its sphere in this way, it usurps power that properly belongs to another institution. This petty tyranny is, of course, the first sign of Leviathan rising.

Christianity has other resources beside the distinction between church and state, civil society, and sphere sovereignty that act as a bulwark against the totalitarian impulses of government. One of the most important is the doctrine of original sin. And this brings us to Augustine of Hippo, the most important theologian in the Latin Christian tradition and the first to highlight original sin and to explore its implications for society and politics.

CHAPTER 2
AUGUSTINE

Never was a government that was not composed of liars, male-factors, and thieves. —MARCUS TULLIUS CICERO (106-43 BC)

In the last chapter, we looked at the issue of separation of church and state and its broader impact on the development of intermediate institutions, civil society, and sphere sovereignty. We noted that when a sphere fails, there is a temptation for the government to step in to fix the problem, but this poses two dangers: first, government is ill-equipped to handle problems in other spheres and often makes the situation worse; second, when government interferes with a sphere outside of its competence, it raises the specter of tyranny and, ultimately, of totalitarianism.

But why is this? Is it not a bit paranoid to see the threat of Leviathan in a government's attempts to regulate areas that do not regulate themselves effectively? Is it really so bad to have government involving itself in businesses, schools, or families that are doing a poor job of governing themselves? The answer is found in the works of St. Augustine.

No church father has had as much of an impact on Western Christianity as Augustine of Hippo (Hippo was a city in modern Algeria). His writings shaped Latin theology throughout the Middle Ages, were a critical part of the Protestant Reformation, and continue to influence theological discussions today. For our purposes, we need to focus on his masterpiece *The City of God*, which is one of the most influential books in history and is responsible for shaping how the Western world thought of itself for well over a thousand years. It was written in the wake of the sack of Rome by the Visigoths in AD 410, the beginning of the end of the Roman Empire in western Europe. Afraid of a fractured future, Roman pagans were arguing that the city fell because it had abandoned its old gods when it adopted Christianity. (Yes, nearly a century after Constantine there were still plenty of pagans in the Empire.) Augustine responded that the problem wasn't that Rome was too Christian, but that it wasn't Christian enough. His lengthy explanation, closing in on half a million words, was the next major development in Christian political theory.

A TALE OF TWO CITIES

The City of God argues that there are two "cities" in this world, the City of Man and the City of God. The City of Man, which Augustine identifies with Rome and other earthly empires, is dominated by self-love and built around self-indulgence, the lowest common denominator in society. Virtue is absent since the citizens of the City of Man love themselves more than others. People may do good things because of social pressure, fear of the state, or some other reason, but ultimately even the good they do is always self-serving and therefore never truly virtuous.

In this environment, the state is necessary to restrain evil. Yet government itself is part of the City of Man and is itself self-serving and dominated by self-love. The state is more interested in self-aggrandizement and power than it is in promoting the good.

At the same time, Augustine believed that government was instituted by God and is therefore potentially good. But because of original sin, in the City of Man government turns away from the good and therefore becomes evil—a necessary evil, in view of the need to restrain vice, but evil nonetheless. In the City of Man, the state is nothing less than organized oppression and maintains its power through coercion, threats, and violence.

The other city in this world is the City of God, which Augustine identified with the New Jerusalem. Where the City of Man is based on self-love, the City of God is characterized by love of God and, therefore, love of neighbor. Because of this focus on other-centered love, all true virtue and all things necessary for human flourishing reside exclusively in the City of God. Only Christians are part of this City, since only they have received the grace to overcome the effects of sin in their lives. Rather than through violence, the City of God achieves its purposes through compassion, mercy, generosity, self-sacrifice, and repentance.

AUGUSTINIAN PESSIMISM

Augustine's ideas about government mirrored his ideas about the human condition: original sin means that we love ourselves rather than God and neighbor, and this selfish love shapes our actions, leading to sin. In government, original sin leads to a lust for power and glory, with the result that Caesar attempts to become lord and sovereign over all areas of life. This is an ongoing temptation for all governments in the City of Man.

Although Augustine paid lip service to the goodness of the Christian emperors, it is also clear that he saw them as being a part of the City of Man, with all the corruption and self-centeredness that entailed. Like any other ruler in the City of Man, they wanted ever-increasing glory and power and thus could not be trusted completely to promote the City of God.

At the same time, government was established by God to perform a good purpose in this fallen world, and thus Christians may participate in it. Further, just as Christ redeems us from sin and makes it possible for us to avoid sin in our personal lives, it is possible for the Christian magistrate to live out and promote the virtues of the City of God while working in and for the City of Man—possible, but very, very difficult.

COOPERATION IN THE CITIES

Even though all human societies need virtue to survive, since they belong to the City of Man, they lack true virtue. The best they can do is to promote a simulacrum of virtue through threat of force. This is one area where the interests of the City of God intersect those of the City of Man. Both cities share an interest in promoting good behavior, though for different purposes and using very different means. The City of Man uses terror—the threat of violence—to compel good behavior and to protect good people from the wicked, whereas the City of God relies only on penitence, grace, and mercy, not compulsion, to advance its goals. Yet despite these differences, the work of each city can complement the other: the magistrate's threat of violence may contribute to the growth of the City of God by encouraging penitence, while the City of God's emphasis on virtue can lead to the stability of the City of Man. Further, the City of God can encourage the City of Man toward the good, though without taking on the responsibility for making laws, while the City of Man can promote good behavior through the courts and can defend society and provide stability to allow the City of God to flourish.

Although this principle extends into other areas, promoting a stable society is a prime example of how the two cities can work together for a common goal but for different ends. The City of Man always seeks stability, if for no other reason than to maintain its own power. This City therefore emphasizes tolerance of differences (as long as they do not undermine the government's power) in order to avoid conflict. To support this, the City of Man legislates only the minimal standards of behavior necessary to preserve a stable society and fiercely represses anything that disrupts stability.

For the City of Man, this passes for peace, despite being distorted by greed and selfishness. The City of God also seeks peace, though of a different and more profound sort. For the City of God, peace means *shalom*, the presence of all things necessary for human flourishing. Among other things, this includes peace and stability within society, and so the City of God and the City of Man can cooperate to some extent in promoting these goals.

Augustine's efforts to find common ground between the City of God and the City of Man provided an important theological justification for Christians to be involved in civil government: by promoting true goodness and virtue as a civil magistrate, the Christian can in fact work to advance the interests of both cities simultaneously. Unfortunately, there was a dark side to Augustine's thinking on cooperation between the cities.

RELIGIOUS COERCION

Augustine took a major step backward from Lactantius and other early Christian writers when it came to religious liberty. As we saw in chapter 1, the early Christians argued for religious liberty on the grounds that for worship to be acceptable to God, it had to be freely given. Augustine agreed with that principle for pagans and Jews, but not when it came to heretics.

The specific issue involved Donatism. About a century before Augustine, prior to the conversion of Constantine, the Emperor Diocletian conducted the Great Persecution, the most brutal crackdown on Christians in Roman history. The politics of this need not concern us here; what is significant is that some Christian leaders gave over Scriptures to be burned or compromised in other ways to avoid torture or execution. One who did not was the Berber bishop Donatus. When the persecution ended, Donatus argued that *traditores*—priests and bishops who had knuckled under in any way during the persecution—demonstrated that they were never true priests to begin with. This meant that any sacraments that they had ever performed were invalid. The only way they could be readmitted to the priesthood was if they confessed their sin to a bishop who had not given in to persecution and then did penance.

When a bishop who was allegedly a *traditor* consecrated a new bishop for Carthage in 311, Donatus and his supporters objected and consecrated a rival bishop. When the Donatist bishop died, Donatus himself replaced him. This set up a schism in the church. The Donatists appealed to Constantine, who asked Pope Miltiades (another Berber) to settle the matter. He ruled against the Donatists, who again appealed to Constantine. After two more rounds of this, the Donatists began rioting. In 316, Constantine responded by threatening death to anyone who disturbed the peace, including by rebaptizing people—a characteristic Donatist practice. He then ordered the confiscation of Donatist church property. Donatus refused to turn over his church, and so it was taken back by force by Roman troops.

The Donatists persisted, however. Some of them allied with the Circumcellions, a radical and at times violent Christian sect in North Africa. As a result, when Rome cracked down on the Circumcellions, they went after the Donatists as well.

This is the context for Augustine's work against the Donatists. On a theological level, he disputed the basic premise of Donatism, that priests had to be faultless as a precondition for their prayers and sacraments to be effective. Instead, Augustine argued that it was the completed work of Christ, not the work of the priest, that made the sacraments effective.[1] But he went beyond this. He also argued that it was perfectly appropriate for the government to coerce heretics to rejoin the orthodox church. He defended this scripturally by citing Luke 14:23, where the master tells the servants to "compel them to enter." Augustine argued that since returning heretics to orthodoxy was a good thing, using coercion to accomplish this was also good.[2]

This was a fateful move on Augustine's part, one which would have long-lasting consequences for church-state relations. It set a precedent for the state to become the church's enforcer, opening the door to heresy trials and executions, wars of religion, and using the tools of the City of Man to limit or eliminate religious liberty. It also served to tie church and state more closely together, complicating the task of

1. This distinction is made in Latin by saying that the sacraments are made effective *ex opere operato* (out of the work that has been done) rather than *ex opere operando* (out of the work that is being done).

2. Augustine, Letter 93 to Vincentius, available online at https://earlychurchtexts.com/public/augustine_letter_93_to_vincentius_cogite_intrare.htm.

drawing boundaries and distinguishing between the responsibilities of the two institutions. Though Augustinian pessimism toward government would have a positive effect on human rights and liberty in medieval Europe and beyond, his support of religious coercion (though not forced conversion) would lead to persecution, wars, and judicial murder well into the seventeenth century.

THE AUGUSTINIAN STATE

The City of God's effect on political thought was especially profound as it promoted a skeptical attitude toward government as an institution and toward government officials. Both are affected by original sin, both are self-serving and self-aggrandizing, both want to accumulate more and more power for themselves, and both are given to abusing the power that they have. All of this implies that government and governors cannot be trusted, and that limiting government with systems of checks and balances is essential to prevent the government from becoming tyrannical.

This thinking shaped legal theory and much of the practice of secular government in medieval Europe. Contrary to common stereotypes, medieval government was not absolutist or built on the divine right of kings; these were much later ideas. Rather, medieval governments were always limited, with no one ruler holding absolute power: Kings ruled under law, with royal councils and frequently various forms of representative bodies acting as checks on their authority to act unilaterally. Although the details varied from state to state, medieval governments all had built-in systems of checks and balances to prevent anyone from having unlimited power.

The Augustinian answer to how a Christian should view the government, then, is quite simple: we should be wary of it, constantly aware of the danger of corruption, and constantly evaluating whether our rulers are people of integrity and virtue. If they are not, we can count on them working to accumulate more power to themselves and sooner or later demanding allegiance to themselves over allegiance to God.

THE CHURCH AND THE CITY OF GOD

If the state is part of the City of Man, where do we find the City of God in this world? The most obvious place to look would be the church. This finds some support in Augustine, who clearly had a high ecclesiology. A number of his writings echo Cyprian's dictum that "Outside the church there is no salvation." At the same time, however, it is not clear that Augustine was referring to the institutional church. In his *Tractates on the Gospel of John*, he commented about the church, "how many sheep are outside, how many wolves within!"[3] He thus had a conception of the Church that went beyond the hierarchical church of his day. Later Protestant theologians developed his thinking on this point into the distinction between the visible and invisible church. Perhaps because of his awareness of the weaknesses of the visible, institutional church

---

3.   Augustine, Tractate 45 (John 10:1-10), available online at http://www.newadvent.org/fathers/1701045.htm.

and the fallible, sinful people in it, Augustine never explicitly identified the church with the City of God.

Others were not so hesitant, however.

Pope Gelasius I (492–496), the last Berber pope, took Augustine's ideas in *The City of God* in new directions. In a letter to the Eastern Emperor Anastasius I Dicorus, Gelasius argued that the church (headed by the Bishop of Rome) is the earthly representative of the City of God and thus is the repository of righteousness, justice, and virtue in the world. But since in this age the church must deal with a great many worldly concerns, the pope can delegate some of his authority over secular matters to the emperor as the head of the state. The emperor is then responsible to handle temporal affairs in subordination to the pope. The implications of this are clear: by extension, all earthly rulers are answerable to their ecclesiastical superiors, who are themselves subordinate to the pope.[4]

Political theorists term this the two swords theory: God has given two swords to the church, the greater for sacred jurisdiction, the lesser for secular jurisdiction. The church lends the lesser sword to the state while retaining the greater, and thus has authority over secular rulers in addition to its spiritual responsibilities.

This was a bold and essentially unprecedented claim. As we have seen, Constantine called the Council of Nicaea to settle the Arian question, as well as synods to deal with Donatism; he did not just submit the issues to the decision of the pope.

---

4. Available online at https://sourcebooks.fordham.edu/source/gelasius1.asp.

Although Ambrose called out Theodosius over the slaughter at Thessalonica, that was an issue of sin on the emperor's part. Ambrose never claimed to have authority over Theodosius in secular matters. Although we do not know Anastasius's reaction to Gelasius's letter, it is difficult to imagine that he took the argument too seriously.

The decision also put him at odds with his fellow metropolitan bishops in Alexandria, Antioch, and Constantinople. The Council of Nicaea had given the metropolitan bishops jurisdiction over the churches in their territory. It explicitly preserved their customary privileges and did not place them under Roman jurisdiction.[5] Gelasius's claim to supremacy over the whole church and thus over the state has thus been rejected to this day by the Eastern Orthodox patriarchs and the Coptic pope in Alexandria, who follow the older tradition of the church as found in Canon 6 of the Council of Nicaea.

More than this, though, the identification of the City of God with the Roman Church is also dangerous. Since sin and corruption are characteristic of the City of Man but not of the City of God, if the Roman Church is the earthly manifestation of the City of God, its decisions should likewise be without sin or corruption. This is what the Catholic Church has periodically claimed through its history. Yet this claim is at odds with the history of the church. The City of God is not self-serving, self-aggrandizing, corrupt, or power hungry, but there have been periods when these things have characterized the Roman Church at its highest levels. And as we have

5. Available online at https://www.csun.edu/~hcfll004/nicaea.html.

seen, Augustine himself recognized that there are wolves in the church. Further, Gelasius's claim, however sincere, suggests that he believed the papacy should have the kind of unlimited power that no human being in a fallen world other than Jesus himself should have.

Augustine's legacy is complex, including both limited government and checks and balances on the one hand, and blurring the lines of responsibility between church and state and interfering with religious liberty on the other. The latter was made far more serious by Gelasius's adaptation of Augustine's ideas, which inverted the pagan Roman world's subordination of religion to the emperor. It did not settle matters, however, and church and state would continue to struggle to define the proper boundaries between them for centuries, even up to the present day. In the next chapter, we will look at how the two sides jockeyed for position with each other over the next seven hundred years.

IMPLICATIONS

Although we usually think of the doctrine of original sin in personal terms, it has much broader application than simply a single person's tendency to sin. Rather, Sin (with a capital *S*) is a principle that infects all areas of human life. Because we are corrupt and corruptible, Sin can embed itself in even the best of our institutions, turning them into vehicles for our own power or pleasure. This is particularly true of government. In the words of Lord Acton's famous dictum, "Power tends to corrupt; absolute power corrupts absolutely."

This means that we must keep a close eye on the institutions that wield power in society. In this chapter, we have focused on government, and given its power, that is certainly a major area of concern. Politicians, political parties, branches of government, regulatory agencies, the judiciary—all are subject to corruption and can be (and are being) used for self-seeking and unjust purposes.

But the state is not the only institution that has power in our society. Think about the role of schools in forming the worldview of the next generation, because that is what they are self-consciously trying to do. The secular education establishment wants to promote a particular set of values to the next generation, values shaped by the sexual revolution and progressive culture, and they want to do it free from the interference or even the knowledge of parents. Sin always flourishes in the dark.

Or consider the media, which openly promote a similar agenda as the schools, slipping in messages that bypass our filters because we are supposed to just sit back and enjoy the entertainment. The media have been an unusually potent force in shaping the moral imagination and changing the values of society.

Contrary to Gelasius I, churches are also subject to the effects of original sin. We see this in many places, from the vast numbers of evangelical pastors who have fallen into sexual sin to the financial improprieties and the child abuse scandals in the Catholic Church.

Sin even infects our families through abuse, absent fathers, lack of proper parenting of children, and a myriad of other ways. And in this case, the sins of the fathers are very directly visited upon the children, creating multiple generations of dysfunction.

The fact of the matter is we are in a time of great tension in society, and that tension is caused by Sin operating personally, institutionally, and corporately. If we as Christians are to take a clear-eyed view of our situation, we need to recognize the reality of Sin in ourselves and its potential to infect everything around us—including government and politics.

This is why we cannot rely on government to deal with our Sin, because government itself is subject to Sin and is ill-equipped to solve social problems outside its proper purview. Instead, we need to use the tools of the City of God—love, compassion, mercy, self-sacrifice, confession, penitence, and the like—to identify Sin in ourselves and in our institutions and to work toward renewing them and restoring them to their proper functions under God. This won't solve all of our problems, of course, but it's where we need to start.

CHAPTER 3
CHURCH, STATE, AND THE LIMITS OF POWER

The argument now that the spread of pop culture and consumer goods around the world represents the triumph of Western civilization trivializes Western culture. The essence of Western civilization is the Magna Carta, not the Magna Mac. The fact that non-Westerners may bite into the latter has no implications for their accepting the former. —SAMUEL P. HUNTINGTON (1927-2008)

Although Augustine would continue to shape political theory in Europe throughout the Middle Ages, ideas derived from Aristotle would provide an important counterweight to Augustinian pessimism about government. To understand why, in this chapter we will look at the evolution of church-state relations beyond the early church, providing the intellectual context for Europe's recovery of Aristotle's works.

CHURCH AND STATE IN THE MIDDLE AGES

The complex relationship between church and state that began in the Roman Empire continued into the Middle Ages in both the eastern and western halves of the empire.

In the eastern half of the empire, which initially included Italy, church and state generally cooperated with each other: the state protected the church and performed the usual run of government responsibilities, and the church handled the sacraments and promoting morality. There were conflicts between the two, but generally the relationship was cordial.

The first serious problem between church and state in the East was the Iconoclastic Controversy. Perhaps due to the influence of Islam, which had taken much imperial territory during the previous decades, Emperor Leo III concluded that the church's use of icons was idolatrous, and he moved to ban them. The patriarch in Constantinople objected, with the support of the pope in Rome. The emperor responded by deposing the patriarch and withdrawing military protection from the pope at a point when he was under threat from the Lombards, an Aryan tribe that had moved into northern Italy. The pope was thus forced into an alliance with the Franks, the first Germanic tribe to convert to orthodox Christianity and a growing power in the Latin world.

Whatever the merits of the argument theologically, this was the first time that the government tried to dictate how worship was to be conducted in Christian churches. Ultimately, the imperial side would lose, with the effect that church and state cooperation was restored in the Eastern Empire. But the emperor's role as papal protector was lost, which would help set up the eventual division between Rome and the Eastern Orthodox Church.

The situation in the Latin-speaking West was far more complicated. During the late fifth and early sixth centuries, Roman authority was collapsing in Western Europe. The bishops in the churches were the only ones left who were capable of handling administrative roles in the cities, and as a result, the bishops became part of the civil government as new states developed in the former Roman Empire.

The kingdom of the Franks was the most important of the barbarian successor states in the Latin half of the old Roman Empire. While the history of the Franks is interesting and colorful, for purposes of this book we need to note only a few things. First, the papal alliance with the Franks facilitated a change in dynasty in the Frankish kingdom from the Merovingians to the Carolingians. Under Charlemagne, the greatest of the Carolingians, the relationship of church and state became a central issue due to a series of events that seesawed between the state having authority over the church and the church having authority over the state, setting precedents that continued to influence politics all the way into the nineteenth century.

The troubles began with the election of Pope Leo III (not the same as Emperor Leo III, who started the Iconoclastic Controversy) in 795. He was from a modest background and was resented by the Roman nobility. Leo prudently sent

Charlemagne a letter informing him of his election; Charlemagne responded by congratulating him and telling him that Charlemagne's role was to run things and Leo's was to pray for him.

In 799, Leo was attacked and nearly killed in the streets, but Charlemagne had troops in Rome who rescued him. When he recovered, he traveled to Charlemagne's court, but his enemies sent messages to Charlemagne accusing Leo of heinous crimes. This posed a problem for Charlemagne: the only person who had a right to judge the pope was the emperor, but that office was held by the Empress Irene, who was a woman and arguably a usurper. It was not clear that Charlemagne had jurisdiction to try the pope, but nonetheless Charlemagne convened a court in Rome, and on December 23, 800, he acquitted Leo of the charges against him.

This set a precedent that the king of the Franks had authority to sit in judgment over the pope, making the king the higher office.

Two days later, after Christmas Mass, Leo approached Charlemagne with a crown in hand and crowned him Roman emperor. Contemporary accounts say Charlemagne was furious: not only did it create diplomatic problems with the Eastern Empire, but since Leo had crowned him, that meant Leo had the authority to make emperors, thus declaring papacy to be the higher office.[1] Charlemagne spent the rest of his reign

---

1. This is the precedent Napoleon Bonaparte had in mind when he had the pope bring him the crown, but took it from the pope and crowned himself emperor of France: he knew the problems that came from Charlemagne's coronation, and he did not want there to be any question of the pope having authority over him.

showing the pope who was really boss, and for the most part, the popes were smart enough not to argue the point.

After Charlemagne, the Carolingian dynasty went into decline, as did the papacy. On the one hand, no ruler actually had enough authority to make a credible claim to the title of emperor, so it stopped being used; on the other hand, the papacy was not in any better shape. The level of corruption in Rome was staggering. For example, Pope Stephen VI had his predecessor, Formosus, exhumed, put in papal robes, propped up in a chair, and tried for heresy (the Cadaver Synod, AD 897). Since Formosus did not offer an effective defense, he was convicted, stripped of his robes, and his body was thrown into the Tiber River. Stephen's successor, Theodore II, revoked the condemnation, fished Formosus's body from the river, and reinterred him. That decision was reversed by Pope Sergius III.

Speaking of Sergius III (904–911), as pope, he took his cousin's 15-year-old daughter Marozia as a concubine; she bore him the future Pope John XII. After this, Marozia was married and bore her husband a son, Alberic; two of Alberic's sons and one of his grandsons also became popes. Marozia effectively ruled Rome and the papacy by guile and sexual favors, which earned the period the title of the papal pornocracy, a word meaning government by prostitutes.

In the mid-tenth century, Otto I became the East Frankish king and began to clean things up. He consolidated his power with the help of reform-minded bishops whom he appointed as key figures in his administration. From there, he moved into Italy, where he deposed a corrupt pope and appointed a reformer as a replacement. Otto was soon recognized as emperor, and he and his successors, Otto II and Otto III, continued to appoint qualified reformers to the papacy.

The reformers, however, began to chafe at the influence of the emperor over the papacy. Through a combination of legal changes that in principle guaranteed the independence of papal elections, disciplinary actions including excommunication of clergy who followed kings rather than papal directions, and military alliances, the papacy gained its independence from the emperor and the Roman mob alike, and eliminated many of the abuses that had plagued it. From there, popes increasingly began to go back to Gelasius I's ideas and began asserting authority over political rulers, including the emperor.

The tension between pope and emperor had been festering for some time, but the issue that brought the conflict into the open was lay investiture of bishops, that is, political authorities (i.e., laymen) vesting bishops with the ring and crozier, which are the symbols of a bishop's spiritual office. This was a consequence of bishops fulfilling roles in secular government and thus being appointed by emperors, kings, and dukes, rather than being elected by the canons of the cathedral with the approval of the pope. From the emperor's perspective, the bishops were part of his administration, so he had the right to choose them; the pope's response was that the bishops were primarily ecclesiastical officers, so they needed to be selected by the church.

Who gets to give a bishop the symbols of his office may seem like a trivial issue, but underlying it was the question of primacy between church and state: was the church over the state, as Gelasius had declared, or was the emperor over the church, following Constantine (who called the Council of Nicaea) and Charlemagne? (Of course, this argument conveniently ignored the Eastern Emperor in Constantinople.) This dispute pitted the bishops' loyalty to the church against their loyalty to the state. The conflict was long and difficult, with excommunications, depositions, and open warfare on both sides. Eventually, an accommodation was reached in the Concordat of Worms (1122), which recognized the claims of both sides, with precedence determined more by proximity to the papal or imperial court than by any political or theological considerations.

Throughout the conflict, both sides recognized that both church and state were ordained by God and given specific responsibilities. The real question was the boundary between them—the age-old question of what belonged to Caesar and what to God: Could the emperor depose immoral popes? Could the pope depose emperors who did not stand for righteousness? Both sides mustered biblical and historical arguments, and both had important theologians who supported them.

But the controversy extended well beyond just the rights of pope and emperor. The Catholic Church claimed other legal rights and responsibilities that did not always sit well with civil governments. For example, members of the clergy (which in the Middle Ages included university students) could only be tried in church courts, not secular courts. Further, issues related to sacraments and other religious actions could only be adjudicated by church courts. This included anything related to marriage (as a sacrament), but also probate and contract law, since these were tantamount to vows and thus an activity regulated by canon (i.e., church) law. These claims increasingly came under attack in the fifteenth and sixteenth centuries as illicit usurpations of the God-given rights and responsibilities of civil government.

While the conflict between popes and emperors was not constant, it did reemerge regularly throughout the period and continued into the Reformation era.

Questions of limitations on royal authority did not always focus on the relationship of church and state. In the case of the Magna Carta (1215), the primary conflict between the barons and King John of England echoed Augustinian concerns about unrestrained governmental power and sought to set strict limits on what the king could and could not do.

THE MAGNA CARTA

King John was, to put it mildly, an unpopular king. He had lost many of England's territories on the continent, then had raised taxes to try to recover them. After that effort ended in failure, many of the barons of England had had enough. They were fed up with John's unilateral actions to try to fund his failed ambitions, combined with his violations of what they saw as their traditional rights and privileges. As a result, the barons took an oath that they would defend the liberties of the church and of the realm, and they insisted that John confirm the Charter of Liberties issued by Henry

I. John entered negotiations with them, but largely played for time. In 1213, he had made himself a vassal of Pope Innocent III, the most powerful pope of the Middle Ages, and he hoped Innocent would take his side of the conflict. The barons, meanwhile, mobilized their military forces, and John realized he was out of time. On June 10, 1215, he was forced to sign the Magna Carta.

The Magna Carta's final form was negotiated by Stephen Langton, the archbishop of Canterbury. It sought to preserve the liberties of the church by securing the independence of episcopal elections as well as protecting the liberties of the city of London, limiting taxation of the barons without their consent, protecting from arbitrary imprisonment, and the right to a swift trial. It even addressed the rights of serfs in several articles. To guarantee the king's adherence to the terms of the charter, a council of twenty-five barons would monitor his behavior and, if he did not address a violation of the charter within forty days of being notified about it, the twenty-five barons were authorized to seize his castles and other properties until he complied with their demands.

Like Henry I's Charter of Liberties, the Magna Carta was based on other legal precedents, including earlier royal charters and even charters from Europe. Although it is considered a landmark in the history of English law, it was never put into effect. Innocent III annulled it as limiting his rights as John's sovereign, and both sides broke the terms of the charter within weeks of its signing. Nonetheless, it was used as a foundation for later charters guaranteeing in

principle the rights of the church, the barons, and much of
the people of England.

A NEW VISION OF POLITICS

To this point, European political thought was dominated by
two trends: the tug-of-war between church and state, and Augustinian pessimism about secular government. Augustine's
City of God, in particular, left the Latin-speaking world with a
view of government that was at best ambivalent: government
was ordained by God and thus potentially good, but given
the reality and pervasiveness of sin, it was inevitably corrupt
and part of the City of Man, a world ruled by selfishness and
self-seeking pride even when led by a Christian emperor. Ex-
amples like John of England reinforced this skepticism about
allowing anyone unrestricted governmental power.

A more positive vision of government came to the medieval
church through the recovery of the writings of Aristotle. Latin
Christian scholars came into contact with previously unknown
texts by Aristotle in Muslim Spain, and they began to translate
them into Latin. These texts revolutionized intellectual life in
medieval Europe, providing a complete and coherent worldview
that addressed many of the critical issues medieval scholars had
been studying. Aristotle's writings were so wide-ranging and so
well thought out that he became known as, in Dante's phrase,
"the master [i.e., teacher] of those who know."

Around 1260, William of Moerbeke translated Aristotle's *Politics* into Latin for the first time, apparently at the
request of Thomas Aquinas. This book is not well known to

the general public today, but it was critically important to the American Founders, helping to shape both what they believed to be the role of government and how they designed the U.S. Constitution. It also provided a new way of thinking about government as a counterpoint to Augustinian pessimism—a task that could only be accomplished by a thinker with the prestige of Aristotle.

POLITICS ACCORDING TO ARISTOTLE

Aristotle's political theory is based on natural law. He argued that the nature of anything is determined by its purpose or, as he put it, its final cause. For humanity, our end is happiness (*eudaimonia*), which he understood to be the full development of all our natural abilities pursued through reason. This leads to a life of virtue and excellence.

In the Declaration of Independence, when Thomas Jefferson wrote of the inalienable right to the pursuit of happiness, this is what he had in mind: since *eudaimonia*, a life of virtue and excellence, is the fundamental purpose of human life, no government can take away our right to pursue it.

Since humanity was created for *eudaimonia*, it follows that human communities are established to help in the pursuit of that purpose. Aristotle saw the state as a largely self-sufficient, self-contained, and therefore complete community. It has as its purpose the promotion of the good in society, which means encouraging its citizens toward a life of virtue. Unlike Augustine, Aristotle thus saw government as performing a positive function in society.

Of course, Aristotle was no fool. He realized that governments do not always tend toward the good, and that they can and do become corrupt. One of his main topics in *Politics* was how to best structure the state to promote its proper end.

Aristotle argued that there were three basic forms of government, each of which existed in both a proper and a deviant form:

1. Rule by a single individual is a *monarchy* in its proper form, but when the monarch rules for self-interest rather than for the common good, it degenerates into a *tyranny*.

2. Rule by a few is an *aristocracy* in its proper form, but it degenerates into an *oligarchy* when the few rule out of self-interest rather than the common good.

3. Rule by many is a *republic* (i.e., rule by representation) in its proper form, and its degenerate form is a *democracy* (literally "mob rule," where the citizens make all decisions directly).

This last seems odd to us today, since we are conditioned to think of democracy as a good thing. But Aristotle, who had lived through Athenian democracy, knew its pitfalls. He recognized what we today describe as mob psychology, that people in crowds act more out of passion than reason. The danger is that a demagogue (literally a "mob leader") would stir the passions of the crowd so that they acted out of emotion, not reason. Since reason is essential for *eudaimonia*, democracy is a degenerate form of government.

Each positive form of government has its strengths and weaknesses. Monarchs can act quickly in a crisis, but if they make a mistake, it can be disastrous. Aristocracies are good at deliberation and so are less likely to make mistakes than monarchies, but they are slow to respond in crises, which can be equally disastrous. Republics have a great deal of buy-in from the citizens, since they feel like they have a say in the government, but republics are, if anything, even slower to respond in the face of crises than aristocracies are.

For Aristotle, the ideal state is one in which all the citizens are virtuous and thus able to participate appropriately in the government. Since most states fall short of this ideal, the next best option is a *mixed state*, where elements of each of the three positive types of government are found and where the balance of power favors neither the rich (which would tend toward oligarchy) nor the poor (which would tend toward democracy) but the people in the middle, whom he believed were more likely to follow the dictates of reason.

APPLYING ARISTOTLE

Although medieval political thought tended to be colored by Augustinian pessimism, Aristotle's positive vision of government had an enormous impact on it as well. This vision found expression in the various attempts to create mixed states across Europe.

- Medieval cities were ruled by a set of representative councils (republic) with a greater concentration of power in smaller councils made up of members of the nobility and wealthy commoners (aristocracy), sometimes with a prince overseeing the whole lot (monarchy).

- Kings (monarchy) ruled with their council (aristocracy) but increasingly had representative parties such as the English Parliament or the Holy Roman Empire's Imperial Diet, which included representation from both the nobility and the commoners (aristocracy and republic). In some ways, this followed intuitions that were already present in medieval governments; for example, the twenty-five barons from the Magna Carta were essentially an aristocratic component in government meant to hold the monarchy in check. (Of course this was proposed forty-five years before Aristotle's *Politics* became available in western Europe.)

- Nobles (monarchy) always ruled with the counsel of their subordinates (aristocracy), who had the right and obligation to advise in matters which affected them.

The Aristotelian view of government was particularly attractive to secular rulers in their conflict with the papacy. Augustine had argued that government was ordained by God and thus could play a positive role in society, though his potent understanding of sin and human corruptibility led him to focus on the negatives. With Aristotle's *Politics*, rulers now had a strong argument for the importance and independence of the secular state to counter Gelasius's assertion of the primacy of the papacy.

Surprisingly, the Holy Roman emperor found support for his independence from and even superiority to the pope among some of the most important theologians in the fourteenth century. The context was Pope John XXII's conflict with Louis of Bavaria, who had been elected Holy Roman emperor over the objections of the pope. Louis was defended by the theologian and philosopher Marsilius of Padua, whose *Defensor Pacis* (1324) attacked the idea that the church had any jurisdiction in the secular world. It argued that Jesus did not have any temporal power and did not intend His church to have any either. Instead, the church should be subordinate to the state in all areas, civil and spiritual. Marsilius made extensive use of Aristotle's *Politics* but went well beyond it by arguing that God gave sovereignty to the *people*. For Marsilius, this meant that the people had the right to elect their leaders, oversee them, and, if necessary, depose them. His system, though republican, thus incorporated a remarkable degree of democracy for the period.

But Marsilius was not the only theologian alienated by John XXII. Francis of Assisi and William of Ockham are both important for our purposes. We will look more closely at this conflict between the Franciscans and the rest of the church and the issue of property rights in the next chapter. However, before we move on, we need to summarize the general trends in medieval political thought, particularly concerning the relationship of church and state. From the days of Pope Gelasius I, church leaders in the Latin world asserted the authority of the church over the state based on an interpretation of *The City of God* that Augustine himself would have rejected. At the same time, in practice, the state frequently dominated the church, appointing bishops and even popes and dictating practice in the churches, despite the distrust of government implied in *The City of God*. During the Central Middle Ages, the Holy Roman emperor and the papacy engaged in a battle over who was superior, involving excommunications, depositions, and sometimes outright warfare. Aside from the conflict between church and state, Augustine's emphasis on limited government and the need for checks and balances influenced the Magna Carta, which sought to limit royal power and ensure the liberties (i.e., rights) of different groups in England. Shortly thereafter, the recovery of Aristotle's *Politics* proved to be an important counterbalance to Augustinian pessimism, providing a theoretical underpinning for the structure of medieval government and strengthening the case for secular authority and the separation of church and state.

IMPLICATIONS

In our modern world with its separation of church and state, the old battle lines of the Middle Ages no longer seem relevant. Institutionally, this is largely the case since religious groups do not have a formal place in government in most first world countries. And yet we do see increasing pressures on churches, ministries, and individuals to conform to a range of government mandates that do not apply to other institutions or assemblies, including when and where they can meet, how many can attend, what they can and cannot do during services, and what policies they have to follow if they are going to continue their ministry. Thus, for example, in some areas Catholic Charities has been given a choice either to place children for adoption with same-sex couples and thereby violate their religious convictions, or to stop facilitating adoptions. This is clearly government interference in the free exercise of religion, yet the attitude of the legislators and regulators is that their concept of civil rights trumps freedom of religion or freedom of conscience.

In other words, the state is increasingly dictating religious practice to the church, effectively inverting the claims of the medieval church to universal jurisdiction.

At the same time, Aristotle reminds us that government is necessary in our fallen world and that it can perform a positive role in shaping society if officials work for the genuine good of the people rather than out of selfish interests, if policy is set by reason not passion, and if the government does not overstep its boundaries by trampling on the liberties of the people. When it fails to do its duty in any of these ways, the government slips from a positive force in society to a negative.

In a republic, it is our responsibility as citizens to use reason, not passion, to determine our votes and to assess whether our officials are using their offices to enrich themselves, whether they make reasoned cases for their positions, how solid their reasoning is, and whether they support or oppose our liberties.

CHAPTER 4
NATURAL RIGHTS
IN THE MIDDLE AGES

There exists a law, not written down anywhere but inborn in our hearts; a law which comes to us not by training or custom or reading but by derivation and absorption and adoption from nature itself; a law which has come to us not from theory but from practice, not by instruction but by natural intuition. I refer to the law which lays it down that, if our lives are endangered by plots or violence or armed robbers or enemies, any and every method of protecting ourselves is morally right.

—MARCUS TULLIUS CICERO (106-46 BC)

The Magna Carta highlights an important concept lurking in the background of political theory in the Middle Ages: the idea of natural rights. This is an idea that has its roots in Roman law and in Stoic and, to a lesser extent, Epicurean philosophy in the ancient world. These ideas about rights evolved considerably during the Middle Ages, primarily based on the musings of the twelfth-century Decretists (i.e., specialists in Gratian's *Decretum*, the primary collection of canon law in the Middle Ages). Theological arguments based on the pronouncements of the Decretists transformed the concept of natural rights from its ancient form to something much closer to modern rights theory. The details of this development are quite complex and frankly unnecessary for the purposes of this study. It will be helpful, however, to sketch the broad outlines of the debates over rights in order to set the groundwork for later ideas about limitations on government power.

A WORD ON TERMINOLOGY

To illustrate the change in meaning of natural rights over time, we should start with the Latin words used in the Middle Ages. The key word is *ius*, which is the root of our words *jurisprudence* and *justice*. (In Latin, *J* and *I* are the same letter.) Its basic meaning is *law*, but it refers not to specific laws but to law in the abstract, to the legal principles or universal laws that are then enacted into legislation. (Our words *legal, legislation*, and the like come from *lex*, the other Latin word for law, which refers to written statutes.)

Ius also refers to rights, though its connection to universal or abstract concepts of law point to a difference in how rights were conceived in the ancient world and how we think of them today. The Stoics believed that the cosmos was governed by *ius*, simultaneously thought of as a universal law and the principles of reason which were binding on all people and which objectively give people certain rights and responsibilities. These do not inhere in individuals, per se, but are part of a larger law external to the individual.

The Stoic emphasis on reason was an important element of the definition of *ius*, whether understood as law or rights. Whatever reason showed to be necessary for human life and for the proper functioning of society was considered a requirement of natural law or a natural right.

FOUNDATIONS: THE DECRETISTS

These concepts provide the starting point for discussions about rights in the *Decretum Gratiani*. The *Decretum*, formally entitled *A Concordance of Discordant Canons*, was a collection of church laws (canons) assembled by Gratian in the twelfth century that identified apparent contradictions amongst them and proposed resolutions for these contradictions. The *Decretum* quickly became the basic textbook for studies of canon law, and thus, in keeping with the academic method of the day, rapidly attracted commentaries by scholars known as the Decretists.

Gratian's work included texts that dealt with rights (*ius*) informed by the Roman and Stoic ideas that, in Christianized form, dominated the worldview when the canons were written. For example, life is a gift from God, so the right to life recognized by the Stoics became unalienable: since life comes from God, no one can deprive us of it arbitrarily, including ourselves. Suicide is thus forbidden, and we must do everything in our power to preserve our lives. To take this further, the Decretists accept capital punishment for serious crimes such as murder, but they raise the question, if you are condemned to death, what are your responsibilities to protect your own life? Their conclusion is that, since the right to life is unalienable, you have a moral responsibility to attempt to escape if possible, as long as you do not need to kill your guards to do so. Similarly, if you are starving and you need food to survive, taking it from someone who has a surplus is a moral duty if it is necessary to preserve your own life.[1] And since law (*lex*) is to be based on *ius*, taking that bread is not a crime, since it is required by our responsibilities before God and the moral law. In fact, the Decretists argued that the starving person has a right (*ius*) to the bread.[2]

The right to life is a good example of what legal historians refer to as an objective right: it is objective in the sense that it exists outside of ourselves and is unalienable. If it were a sub- jective right—a personal possession—then we would be able to renounce it by committing suicide or allowing ourselves to starve or to be executed.

LIBERTY

The concept of rights in the Decretists is closely connected to liberty (Latin *libertas*). The original term originally referred to a zone of freedom of action within the boundaries of law

---

1. Taking it from someone who would then be in danger of starvation is not permissible.
2. The idea of property rights, which might compete with this, had not yet emerged.

(*ius* and *lex* both). Anything that is neither required nor prohibited by law we are free either to do or not do according to our own choices and decisions. Liberty is thus a right as well, since it exists within the framework of *ius*.

In this context, liberty is a broader concept than we usually consider it. In the Middle Ages, it applied not simply to individuals but also to corporations. Thus, the church had liberties—it was free to operate as it willed within a legally defined set of boundaries. Towns had liberties defined by their charters—legal documents that outlined their rights and privileges. Guilds also had liberties. So did individuals, of course, but it is easy for a modern person to overlook the corporate dimension of liberty as understood in the Middle Ages.

And this concept of rights and liberty brings us back to the Magna Carta. It included protection for the liberties of the church and the city of London as corporate entities, but also protection for the liberties of the barons individually and collectively, of free men, and even of serfs. For the most part, these were affirmations in positive law of liberties that these groups had traditionally held or that had been granted in earlier royal decrees. This means that these rights and liberties were not simply an expression of *ius* as universal law or as reason applied to society's needs. Rather, the Magna Carta guaranteed a number of civil liberties, that is, liberties rooted in the law of the kingdom, rather than natural liberties such as the right to life. While liberty in the abstract is an unalienable right under natural law and the law of God, these liberties are of a different sort, with roots in the specific historical and legal context of England in the early 1200s. In general, they refer to limited autonomy guaranteed to certain corporations within the kingdom. And, since we are dealing with freedom to act within set boundaries established by law or tradition, this meets the classic definition of *liberty*. For example, the "liberties" of the city of London include all the rights granted to the city under its charter, such as the right to elect its own mayor. The Magna Carta prevents the city's charter or any of the liberties it contains from being revoked by the crown. Although there are parallel documents in other areas of Europe, no one confused the specific rights and liberties granted in these charters with universal rights, natural rights, or, to use modern terminology, human rights.

During the thirteenth century, rights discourse began a slow shift away from objective rights to subjective rights, that is, rights that are powers or possessions of an individual rather than an expression of abstract law. The critical element was the development of the concept of property rights, ironically enough first articulated by Franciscans attempting to defend their right to renounce possessions.

THE FRANCISCANS AND PROPERTY RIGHTS

To understand the emergence of the idea of property rights, it will be helpful to discuss the early history of the Franciscans, mentioned briefly last chapter. Francis of Assisi was the son of a wealthy merchant living in an era of increasing prosperity in Europe. This was also an era of religious discontent, with a wide range of reform movements that almost invariably took aim at the wealth and power of the Catholic

Church. If you were a poor shepherd barely keeping your family alive, it was easy to resent the bishop in his jeweled vestments eating off gold plates who forced you to pay him a tithe of your meager earnings. But along with the natural resentment of the rich getting richer on the backs of the poor, the age was also characterized by a kind of salvation anxiety brought about by growing prosperity: Jesus said blessed are the poor and pronounced woe on the rich; He also said it was easier for a camel to go through the eye of a needle than for a rich man to enter the kingdom of Heaven. What, then, did that mean for the people who were getting wealthier during the Middle Ages? Could they be saved?

This was the context of Francis's conversion and was at the core of his reform program. He taught apostolic poverty—the idea that Jesus and the apostles renounced all possessions and owned nothing—and made it a fundamental principle in his order. The Franciscans were mendicants who were to beg for their daily needs. The gifts were to be given in kind rather than in cash as a way of following Jesus's example and teaching of living by faith. Money could only be accepted for immediate needs that could not be met by begging.

Francis was enormously popular and soon attracted a large following across Europe. Even during his lifetime, however, members of the order began compromising on some of his ideals. For example, they argued that people could donate property to the papacy for the use of the Franciscans. That way, the Franciscans could use it without owning it, a distinction that would become increasingly important over time. Francis himself thought that these compromises violated the spirit of his rule, but he was unwilling to assert leadership over his own order, and these practices became widespread among the Franciscans. Near the end of his life, Francis wrote his Spiritual Testament, in which he criticized the direction the order had taken and called it back to his ideals.

After Francis's death, his successor as leader of the order began raising funds to build a great basilica in Assisi to house Francis's remains. The stricter party within the order opposed this as a complete violation of all of Francis's rule. The tensions that had existed even in Francis's lifetime between the Franciscans who wanted to follow Francis's Spiritual Testament (later known as the Spirituals) and those who wanted a laxer interpretation of the rule (later known as the Conventuals) thus came to the fore.

For a time, the stricter party had the support of most of the popes. John XXII, however, supported the laxer Franciscans and thought the arguments for strict apostolic poverty among the Spirituals were ridiculous. He argued that when dealing with consumables, it is absurd to say that someone can use them without owning them. For example, if I use a piece of bread that someone gave me so that it no longer exists when I am done eating it, in what sense can it be said that I did not own the bread? Once I accept the bread, particularly with the intent of consuming it, I own it in any meaningful sense of the word. And since Franciscans have an unalienable right to life and thus to the food necessary to sustain it, they must have an unalienable right to ownership of the food they consume. Thus, apostolic poverty is a false doctrine, and so John XXII declared it heretical.

Needless to say, the Spiritual Franciscans went ballistic. As noted previously, this drove the Spiritual Franciscans into the arms of John XXII's political opponent, Louis of Bavaria, and led them to develop a theory of property rights in order to affirm their right to renounce ownership.

OCKHAM AND *DOMINIUM*

Although other Franciscans attempted to respond to John XXII, the most important defense of apostolic poverty was William of Ockham. Ockham was a nominalist theologian in England, but although scholars have argued that his views on rights depended on his nominalism, his arguments on rights came from canon law and the Decretists rather than from his metaphysical ideas.

Through the thirteenth century, there was no consensus on the origin of property. Most lawyers and theologians argued that there was no property in Eden—so where did property come from after the Fall? Was it purely a matter of human law, or did it have divine origin? If so, where and when? Or was it a matter of *ius* in the sense of what right reason tells us is good and necessary for society?

Prior to Ockham, the Franciscan Bonagratia argued with the majority of canonists that prior to the Fall, there was no property, and everyone had free use of whatever they needed. He argued that Christ and the apostles returned to this state of innocence, owning no property but having usufruct (the right to use and enjoy) of what they needed. Against this, John XXII argued that in Eden, Adam and Eve held all things in common, but prior to Eve, Adam had sole personal ownership of all things. This, the pope argued, was granted by God in the dominion Adam was commanded to exercise over the earth. (The Latin *dominium* refers to both ownership and rule.) So, private property was instituted by God; and although Jesus and the apostles did return to the state of innocence, this was through both individual and common ownership. Thus, the true apostolic lifestyle (which was sought by the Franciscans) does not involve repudiation of all ownership.

Ockham's response to John XXII developed over time. Initially, he was concerned overwhelmingly with the issue of property and poverty. He took on John XXII's arguments point by point: 1) Adam's grant of *dominium* must have included Eve because it was tied to "reproduce and multiply" in the text (Gen. 1:28). 2) Even if it was given prior to Eve, it was obviously given to Adam *and his wife and descendants.* 3) *Dominium* here does not mean ownership but rulership under God over the creation. 4) God gave Adam and Eve use of herbs and fruit to supply the necessities of life, but not ownership of them.

So what was the origin of property? Ockham argued that it came from people moving into unoccupied lands—in Ockham's words, "What no one owns is conceded to the occupier." This means that property was not granted by God individually or in common; rather, it was a human invention dictated after the Fall by our use of reason, part of the ancient definition of *ius*. God later made use of this in granting land to the Israelites, for example, but since property is established in its origin by humanity and is regulated by human law, it is licit to renounce our right to it. We cannot renounce life and the use of food and other necessities, but we can renounce possessions.

Surprisingly, given his argument that property did not exist in the state of innocence, Ockham also rejected John XXII's argument that the pre-Fall state was normative and that Jesus and the Apostles lived in alignment with it. Rather, Ockham claimed that Adam's *dominium* was unique. So Jesus and the apostles did not return to the pre-Fall state but operated in a world in which reason had granted a renounceable right to property. They thus did renounce ownership, using what was necessary but owning nothing. This was the lifestyle that the Franciscans aspired to.

As time went on, Ockham modified his argument about property to support Louis of Bavaria's right to the title of Holy Roman emperor in the face of papal opposition. Papal supremacists argued that all authority on earth is vested in the pope as the vicar of Christ, and thus that there is no legitimate *dominium* apart from the true church and authorization by the papacy. Ockham countered that God himself granted property and rulership directly to humanity, and thus that they exist apart from the papacy. Even pagan rulers have legitimate jurisdiction over their countries: Both the right to property and the right to establish rulers were supported by right reason as things that are good and necessary for society to flourish.

This later stand by Ockham contradicted elements of his earlier arguments, but it maintained the key element that Franciscans could renounce ownership: he draws a distinction between the right to appropriate property and to establish governments on the one hand, and the actual ownership of property and the authority to rule on the other. Ockham's distinction between appropriation and ownership was particularly important for property rights. In later centuries, his distinction between establishing government and ruling would become important in conjunction with Protestant resistance theory and the right of revolution.

PROPERTY RIGHTS AND SUBJECTIVE RIGHTS

Ockham's work on property rights did two things simultaneously. First, in a bid to defend the Franciscans' right to renounce property, it established property as a God-given right, albeit of a different sort than the right to life. The right to life imposes obligations: you must do everything in your power to preserve it. Property rights, much like the right to establish governments, are different. Property ownership can be renounced and property alienated without touching the right to property itself just as governments can be changed without touching the right of the people to establish a government.

In conjunction with the second point, Ockham established a firm foundation for subjective rights, that is, rights that are a power (*potentas*) of an individual. To summarize: rights were originally seen as objective, rooted in natural law external to the individual. After the twelfth century, there was a gradual shift toward a more subjective concept of rights. Ockham essentially completed this process by giving the first clear and coherent explanation of subjective rights. This would become the norm among legal theorists from the fifteenth century to the early modern period.

Property rights would also feature in the continuing evolution of legal and political theory, though Europe had a long tradition of honoring property and inheritance rights in ways that other cultures did not. A striking example of this comes from a few centuries later. At the Battle of Lepanto (1572) between the Ottoman fleet and a coalition of Catholic forces in the Mediterranean basin, when the Turkish commander Ali Pasha's galley was captured, his entire personal fortune was found on board. Ali Pasha had to carry his treasure with him because, if he displeased the sultan, it could have been confiscated if it were within the sultan's reach. No Christian commander needed to worry about arbitrary confiscation of his property. In Europe, a person's property might be confiscated if convicted of treason in a court of law, but in almost any other circumstance, property rights were secure.

IMPLICATIONS

Medieval thinkers recognized that the right to life was unalienable: since life came to us directly from God, we do not have the right to take it from anyone, even ourselves. Suicide is thus self-murder, the unlawful taking of human life. The right to property is likewise unalienable, though since the things we receive do not come to us directly from the hand of God, we are free to buy, sell, give away, and even renounce specific items of property without touching the right to ownership itself.

But what about liberty? Is that something we can legitimately renounce? Medieval theologians do not directly address the question, though in view of Aquinas's rejection of slavery as a violation of natural law, they would likely argue that liberty is a direct gift of God, and thus we do not have the right to renounce it or surrender it. (Locke would argue this explicitly in the seventeenth century.)

So no one can legitimately take our liberty from us nor can we voluntarily surrender it. But can we treat it like property? According to Ockham, we can renounce ownership but not use of things necessary for survival. In the same way, can we renounce liberty in some areas where it is permitted under divine and natural law if demanded by the state? Since the classic definition of liberty is freedom of action within the boundaries set by natural and divine law and by the state, the answer would seem to be yes. Further, by definition, liberty imposes no necessity on us, so that we are free to act or not as we choose.

On the other hand, since the laws of the state are to conform to natural and divine law, the degree to which such restrictions on our liberty are licit is far from clear. Such laws in effect take away our liberty—we no longer have freedom to choose our actions. To adapt an example from Václav Havel, if a store owner wanted to put up a sign saying, "Workers of the world, unite!" he would be free to do that; it is a matter of liberty. But if the government mandated that he had to put up that sign, it would take away his liberty because it would no longer be an action he freely chose. It would thus destroy the person's God-given liberty even if he would be otherwise willing to put up the sign. And it would absolutely violate the liberty of those who did not want to affirm that slogan.[3]

Further, the analogy to property rights fails. According to Ockham, property can be renounced only because the right to property comes from human reason, rather than divine origin, yet our right to liberty comes from God Himself and is thus unalienable. Understood in these terms, laws that restrict our liberty are illegitimate.

And yet, the laws of nature and nature's God also impose on us obligations to act for the good of our neighbors. Thus, we cannot take a radically individualistic view of our rights. Instead, the law of love suggests that we balance individual freedom with public order and concern for the common good, a concept known as *ordered liberty*. Exactly where to draw the lines between order and liberty is not always clear, and governments frequently get the lines wrong, allowing freedom where it is harmful and restricting liberty where it is not. Despite the difficulties, however, ordered liberty presents the best approach to the responsibilities and rights of a citizen in a properly established state. Liberty thus may be an unalienable right, but it is not an absolute right.

Medieval canon lawyers and theologians recognized the rights to life, liberty, and property—the three fundamental rights that would be identified by John Locke at the end of the seventeenth century. How those rights were understood

---

3. Havel's solution is civil disobedience. For a thorough discussion, see his 1978 essay "The Power of the Powerless," which is available online at https://www.nonviolent-conflict.org/wp-content/uploads/1979/01/the-power-of-the-powerless.pdf.

would change over time, but the roots of Locke's ideas date back to the Central Middle Ages. We will return to later explanations and justifications of these rights in subsequent chapters. For now, we need to turn to developments in political theory during the Reformation.

CHAPTER 5
LAW & GOVERNMENT
IN THE PROTESTANT REFORMATION

A Christian is a perfectly free lord of all, subject to none. A Christian is a perfectly dutiful servant of all, subject of all, subject to all. —MARTIN LUTHER (1483–1546)

Although the Reformation was primarily a religious movement, given the way religion intertwined all aspects of life, it inevitably had implications for law and political theory. To understand those developments, however, we must first briefly outline the beginning of the Reformation and its core ideas.

THE NEED FOR REFORM

Throughout the Middle Ages in western Europe, the Catholic Church was enmeshed in all parts of society. The rhythms of life—birth, coming of age, marriage, death—were all accompanied by sacraments; membership in the community was defined in terms of participation in the Eucharist (which was mandatory for the laity only once per year at Easter); bishops held important positions in government; medical care was often done by clergy; fields were blessed by priests; secular organizations like guilds participated in religious rituals; most formal education on all levels came through the church; and so on. Most importantly, however, it was only through the ministry of the church that you had any hope of attaining heaven. In a world where everyone had to deal with death regularly, where all adults recognized that life was short and eternity long, the prospect of salvation was a matter of immediate, daily concern.

But the church was also corrupt. Clergy from popes down to priests had illegitimate children. Monks were proverbially drunks. Money and power motivated much that happened in the church, especially at higher levels. At lower levels, sometimes parish priests did not even understand the Latin of the Mass that they chanted every day.

And yet the position of the Catholic Church was unassailable since they had a monopoly on the one "product" everyone wanted: salvation. Until that monopoly was broken, no matter how bad the church was, people still had to stay in its good graces if they were to have any hope of heaven.

Reformers such as Erasmus advocated cleaning up the abuses in the church, but entrenched interests kept these critiques from getting enough traction to effect real change. And it really didn't matter: ever since Augustine, the Catholic Church had argued that sacraments worked *ex opere operato*, and thus, no matter how unworthy a priest, bishop, or pope was, as long as he was properly ordained and performed the ritual appropriately, the sacrament still worked: sins were forgiven, bread and wine were transubstantiated, and so on.[1]

Enter Martin Luther.

THE RISE OF PROTESTANTISM

Martin Luther was an Augustinian monk who struggled with an overwhelming sense of guilt before a holy God. He could never find peace or a sense of forgiveness—this despite spending hours upon hours confessing his sins and following the most rigorous practices of monastic piety. Then, one day, as he was reading Augustine and studying the Epistle to the Romans, he had a spiritual breakthrough: he rediscovered Paul's emphasis on justification by grace through faith. God does not demand perfection from us; instead, he

---

1. This view of the sacraments may be part of the reason that the Catholic Church has covered up sexual abuse by the clergy: as duly ordained priests, their sacraments still "worked" even if they abused children. If their sacramental work, the very core of their job, was still valid, why not save the church embarrassment by covering up their misbehavior? Conversely, in 2020 a Catholic priest watching a video of his baptism discovered that the priest who had baptized him had said "We baptize you" instead of "I baptize you." That mistake in the formula rendered his baptism null and void according to his bishop, which meant that none of the other sacraments he had received were valid, including his ordination, which meant none of the sacraments he had performed were valid, including baptisms (at least potentially), absolutions through the sacrament of reconciliation (i.e., penance or confession), marriages, and so on.

supplies what we lack, giving all to us by sheer grace obtained through the death and resurrection of Christ, and all he asks of us in return is that we trust him—another word for having faith. With this "tower experience," Luther was set free from his guilt. It transformed his life, and justification by grace through faith alone became the core doctrine of his theology.

Luther realized that this went against the systems of theology within the Catholic Church at the time, but initially he viewed his ideas as simply a corrective to some wrong emphases within the church. He did not realize at first the extent to which his ideas undermined nearly all aspects of Catholicism. For example, justification by faith alone disassembles almost all of the sacramental system of the Catholic Church and makes it necessary to redefine what is left. To defend his ideas, Luther appealed directly to Scripture, rejecting the authority of the pope and Catholic tradition and thus removing them from their privileged place politically and in society.

The details of this conflict need not detain us here. What we do need to note is that by breaking the Catholic Church's monopoly on the means of grace and thus on salvation, Luther caused a cascade of other effects in every area that the church had been involved in—in other words, across *all* of society. For our purposes, we need to look at Luther's thinking about law and government.

THE USES OF THE LAW

The contrast between Luther's experience with penitential practices in the monastery and the freedom he found in the doctrine of justification by faith alone led him to reject any connection between works and salvation. Later Reformed theologians argued that true faith resulted not only in the forgiveness of sins but inevitably also led to good works; Luther did not agree. Instead, he argued that forgiveness of sins came from faith, but that good works were a separate issue: they were appropriate as an expression of gratitude for salvation and of love for God, but they were not a necessary result of faith. Unlike the law, which is based on obedience, the gospel is based on grace coming to us entirely undeserved from God and operating in our life solely on the basis of faith.

This raises the question, if works are not necessary for salvation, what is the relationship between law and gospel? Luther concluded that, for a Christian, the law served two functions. First, through fear of punishment, the law restrained people from committing evil acts; in this context, *law* would include both the biblical and civil law. Second, biblical law shows us our guilt before our God and so drives us to the gospel.

Lutheran and Reformed theologians after Luther added a third use of the law: it is a guide to right behavior for Christians.[2] For many Lutherans, the point here was that, as a guide to living, the law shows us how far short we fall and continues to drive us to Christ—for them, the third use is an extension of the second use of the law. For the Reformed, however, as a guide to proper living, the law teaches us the good works that should emerge from our faith.

2. There is some debate about whether Luther held to this third use of the Law, but it seems most likely that it came from his protégé and successor Philip Melanchthon.

This didactic function of law recognized by the Reformed is an important function of law today: people very often associate what is legal with what is moral. Legislation thus plays a major role in shaping public morality, a point recognized by the Puritans who established schools in New England so that people would know their Bible and hold their legislatures accountable for the laws that they passed.

TWO KINGDOMS DOCTRINE

The first and second uses of the law were foundational to Luther's understanding of the roles and relationship between church and state. Not surprisingly, Augustine's *The City of God* was also important to Luther, although he modified its argument in important ways.

Luther argued that God had two kingdoms in this world, the right-hand kingdom and the left-hand kingdom. The right-hand kingdom is very similar to the City of God in Augustine and grows out of the second use of the law (showing us our guilt and driving us to the gospel). Those who, through the law, have recognized their sin and responded in true faith to God's offer of forgiveness are part of this kingdom. It is spiritual, invisible, and internal, and it is ruled by the Holy Spirit and grace. There is no need for coercion or violence in this kingdom, since its citizens obey God freely and naturally.

The left-hand kingdom consists of the institutions that God has set in place to govern the visible world. At first glance, this might suggest that the left-hand kingdom corresponds to the City of Man, but Luther differs substantially from Augustine in his discussion of this kingdom. The City of Man represents the world in rebellion against God; the left-hand kingdom operates under divine authority to promote God's purposes in society by fulfilling the first use of the law. In other words, this kingdom is ordained by God to restrain evil by the threat of or, if necessary, by the use of force.

In Luther's day, the Catholic Church wielded a great deal of power politically and legally. Luther was highly critical of the Catholic Church, but he could not completely escape his cultural context with respect to the church's responsibilities in overseeing society. As a result, for Luther, the left-hand kingdom includes not simply the civil government but also the visible church. Luther at this point distinguishes the visible church from the true church, that is, the right-hand kingdom which consisted of all the faithful and was known only to God. The visible church performed a role in the left-hand kingdom by providing religious education and in regulating religious practice. The left-hand kingdom thus corresponds directly to the two swords of Catholic thought (see chapter 2). However, there is an important difference: Luther did not see the state as the lesser sword, placing it under the authority of the church. If anything, Luther did the opposite.

Luther's conception of the church's role in the left-hand kingdom differs in another significant way from the Catholic view current in his day: the left-hand kingdom, including the church, had authority only over external behavior, not over conscience.

At this time, the Catholic Church believed it had the right to enforce its beliefs and practices in society using the full coercive force of both church and state. Thus, inquisitorial courts ferreted out heresy, and the heretics were turned over to the state for execution. Individuals could be excommunicated by the church and incur significant civil and legal penalties as a result, and entire kingdoms could fall under interdict (i.e., mass excommunication) if the king defied the pope. Luther, himself excommunicated from the Catholic Church and subject to summary execution should he be found, did not believe the church had the right to do any of this. Neither church nor state had the authority to bind consciences through demanding adherence to man-made laws, traditions, and practices or by false teaching about works being necessary for salvation. Luther specifically had in mind practices like fasting, clerical celibacy, penance, or any other religious obligation not explicitly mandated by Scripture.

God alone has authority over our consciences, and thus they are bound only to the Scriptures, which sets our consciences free in Christ. Should any earthly power, civil or ecclesiastical, claim authority over our consciences, then we are obligated to disobey that power even at the cost of our lives. We will return to the issue of responding to unjust laws later, but for now it is worth noting that Luther arrived at the early church's position on religious liberty and freedom of conscience, which we discussed in chapter 1, though he came by a different path. Unfortunately, neither Luther nor his successors followed through on this point with any consistency. It would be centuries before almost any region in Europe, including Lutheran territories, would accept true religious liberty, the right to live out your faith without government interference as long as doing so does not violate your neighbor's rights.

STATE CHURCHES

The rise of Protestantism also forced a reconsideration of the relationship of church and state. As we have seen, the early church recognized that church and state were separate institutions thanks to a legacy of three centuries of persecution at the hands of the Roman government. Through the Middle Ages, the pope had claimed universal jurisdiction over all Christians and had a parallel government running alongside secular governments; in practice the civil and ecclesiastical governments often worked hand-in-glove, with bishops holding both secular and religious authority and the pope functioning as the head of an Italian state. After the break with Rome caused by the Reformation, Protestant states needed to come up with a new approach to church-state relations. They certainly were not going to follow the Catholic two-swords argument that placed the state under the authority of the church, a position that secular governments (especially in the Holy Roman Empire) had been resisting for centuries. Luther's doctrine of the Two Kingdoms suggested a solution: since both church and state were part of the left-hand kingdom, they could be brought together through the creation of state churches.

The idea of state churches was not entirely new. For example, both John Wycliffe in the 1300s and Jan Hus in the 1400s had advocated for de facto national churches with greater state control over ecclesiastical affairs. Protestants took this one step further and made the church a branch of the state. In Lutheran areas, the state handled administrative affairs for the church and regulated some aspects of worship and doctrine, but otherwise left the churches to conduct their own business.

ZWINGLI AND REFORMED PROTESTANTISM

An alternate vision for reform came from Zurich under the leadership of Ulrich Zwingli. Although Zwingli is best remembered for his conflict with Luther over the Lord's Supper, for our purposes, his significance is the political context of his reform. To understand why, we need to look at trends in late medieval politics.

Throughout medieval history, with a few exceptions, eighty percent or more of Europeans lived in the countryside. These rural territories were dominated by the feudal nobility, who held land by a grant from a higher noble in return for military service or, increasingly as time went on, for cash payments. Part of the reason for the change to cash was simply that it was more versatile: if you were not having a war, you could spend it on other things, and if you were, you could hire mercenaries. But it was also part of a trend that was transforming the decentralized political system of feudalism toward increasingly centralized monarchies. In this way, the state was following in the wake of the church by concentrating power in the hands of fewer and fewer people at the apex of a political power pyramid. Luther was operating in this context, so he maintained a hierarchical structure in the church through the use of bishops.[3] In Aristotelian terms, church and state both maintained an essentially monarchical structure.

The exceptions to this were the medieval and Renaissance cities. Urban populations were scattered across Europe with concentrations in the Low Countries, northern Italy, and the Rhineland; they were also at the heart of the Swiss Cantons. These cities became self-governing entities in one of two ways. In northern Europe, they typically obtained a charter from the king or emperor which granted them rights and privileges in return for fulfilling a set of responsibilities to the monarchy and in turn defined the rights and responsibilities of the monarch with respect to the town. In northern Italy, it was more common for the town to assert its independence from its overlord as a free commune. To do this, a sworn association of citizens would declare the existence of the commune and establish a committee to draw up a constitution; it would also fortify the town to defend its actions against its rejected overlord. In both cases, the formation of the town thus took the form of a covenant between the ruler and the subjects.

Although some Renaissance cities had a prince as head of state, virtually all cities in the period set up representative governments—in other words, Renaissance cities were republics, though organized on different principles than the ones with which we are familiar today. The body politic was not conceived as a collection of individuals but rather as a

---

3. Lutheran bishops did not have the same type of jurisdiction as Catholic bishops; their roles were primarily administrative, but they did have oversight and a fair amount of authority over the local clergy.

collection of associations and corporations. The most important of these corporations had representation in government.
These included the major guilds that were the lifeblood of
the economic life of these cities. Nobles and other wealthy
families who were not guild members were included as well.

All of this helps make sense of some of the less-discussed
differences between the Lutheran and Zwinglian reforms.
Zwingli's reform began in Zurich, a Renaissance republic.
The Reformation in Zurich had as its starting point the Affair of the Sausages (1522), where members of Zwingli's congregation ate sausages during the Lenten fast. Subsequent
events led to two disputations in 1523, after which the town
council voted in favor of Zwingli's reform program against
the Catholics on the one hand and the radicals led by Conrad
Grebel on the other.

Zwingli's reform thus began with a debate which won over
the populace and the government; proper preaching then educated the people about the true religion, and, as they were
ready, the reform was to progress. The Zwinglian reformation then spread to other cities and cantons (states within the
Swiss confederation) using essentially the same methodolo-
gy: a debate, followed by a vote, and then a process to disciple
the people as Protestants.

Zwingli was a strong biblicist, and, unlike Luther, he put
a great deal of stress on the Old Testament. From the Old
Testament, Zwingli and his followers emphasized the idea
of the covenant, understood primarily in terms of a bilateral
agreement between God and a people in which God agrees
to be their God and they agree to obey him. This bilateral

element led Zwingli to put more emphasis on obedience and godly living than Luther did, but it also led Zwingli to envision the church as a covenant body as well.

All of this was in keeping with the urban focus of the Zwinglian reformation. It echoed the origins of the cities in charters granted by emperors or the original agreements of the citizens to declare their independence, both of which can be conceived as covenants enacted by the will of the people (or at least with their agreement). Not surprisingly, they also adopted systems of church governance that also echoed the structure of the state, with an emphasis on plurality of leadership and church councils drawn from not only the professionals in the clergy but notable citizens as well. This differed sharply from the power pyramid of the larger territorial states that was echoed in Luther's church. In many ways, it was far more in keeping with the constitutionalism and limited government of the Middle Ages and stood in opposition to the incipient absolutism of Lutheran states. That said, the Reformed churches that followed Zwingli rather than Luther set up state churches following the example of the Lutherans. There simply was no other model for church-state relations available to them. True religious liberty would only come later.

CALVIN'S GENEVA

As Zwinglianism spread through about half of Switzerland and into the imperial cities in the Rhineland, local conditions created a range of approaches to church structure.

However, the first coherent and distinctively Protestant system of church government was not surprisingly developed by a highly trained lawyer, John Calvin.

Calvin believed that both church and state were institutions ordained by God, that both had specific responsibilities, and that neither should interfere with the work of the other. Following the principles of government in Renaissance cities, the pastors had their own council—the Venerable Company of Pastors—that acted as a pastoral support group, set up preaching rotations and the like for the churches, examined ministerial candidates, and discussed ecclesiastical issues. In purely civil matters, the pastors could advise the state on issues with moral or religious implications, but they did not have any civil or judicial authority. Similarly, the state had very limited authority in purely ecclesiastical matters. That said, Calvin also made pastors paid civil servants who could be fired on twenty-four hours' notice; in other words, they remained state employees even as Calvin carved out a sphere of independent action for them.

Where church and state responsibilities overlapped in helping the poor and enforcing public morality, the civil and ecclesiastical authorities worked together. Thus, Calvin set up or adapted existing institutions that included representatives of both church and state to handle those areas.

The issue of public morality in Calvin's Geneva deserves some further discussion. Calvin believed that good works were a necessary consequence of saving faith and thus also accepted the third use of the law discussed above. Expanding on Luther's distinctions, Calvin emphasized the law's pedagogical function, teaching us what righteous behavior looks like, since in our fallen state we do not know how to live a holy life. This third use of the law led to an emphasis on church discipline, which dealt with breaches in public morality and failures in religious practice.

Calvin thus set up a council known as the consistory made up of the pastors and lay elders drawn from different parts of the government.

Especially early on, the consistory's primary concern was converting the religious practice of the city from Catholic to Protestant. Thus, the consistory would call people in to quiz them on their religious activities and whether they knew the Lord's Prayer, the Ten Commandments, and the Apostles' Creed in their own language. Like other Protestants, Calvin saw religious education as a legitimate responsibility of the church, though the fact that a mixed church-state institution enforced it suggests that it was not, for Calvin, merely an ecclesiastical function. As the city became more thoroughly Protestantized, the consistory's focus shifted toward what had initially been its secondary concern: dealing with behavior that, while not criminal, nonetheless caused public scandals. This included activities like loud quarreling, being drunk and disorderly, and sexual misconduct, particularly if it resulted in pregnancy and thus became publicly known. As moral issues, these fell under the purview of the church; as disruptions of public life, they were also civil concerns, and thus it required a mixed church-state institution to deal with them.

In keeping with Two Kingdoms doctrine, the consistory did not attempt to bind consciences, that is, tell a person what they must believe beyond what is mandated in Scripture. Instead, the consistory only regulated behavior. They believed that, since only God can see into the human heart, regulating conscience is impossible to mere mortals and thus is outside of the scope of both church and state.[4]

CALVINIST CONTRACT THEORY

Calvin is also given credit for codifying the earlier covenantal view of government. Zwingli and earlier reformers had seen in the Old Testament a covenantal vision of God's relations with humanity; in the context of Renaissance city republics, the idea of covenant was easily transferable to secular government. Calvin developed the argument for covenantal civil government with characteristically thorough and clear biblical argumentation.

The foundation of the argument was the book of Exodus. At Sinai, when God established His covenant with Israel, He asked them three times if they accepted the terms of the covenant; only after they had agreed three times was the covenant ratified. For Calvin, this set two important precedents. First, government was to be based on the consent of the governed, an old medieval principle that Calvin found new warrant for in the biblical text. Second, if even God's rule over Israel was established by covenant, all governments must be established through a covenant between ruler and subjects. Calvin thus provided theological justification for the historic covenantal

---

4. Making sure people knew the Lord's Prayer, Ten Commandments, and Creed was a matter of education to Calvin. It did not bind the conscience.

polity of the Renaissance cities which had converted to Reformed Protestantism. Of course, this also justified the form of popular sovereignty found in them, that is, government by representative councils as established by the founding charters of each city.

In the following decades, the republican principles that Calvin incorporated into his local church structure were expanded into Presbyterian polity, a system of national church government developed by the French Huguenots due to the unusual circumstances facing them in France in the late 1550s. It sat uneasily with the monarchial structure of the civil government of France, leading Catholic propagandists to accuse them during the Wars of Religion of being antimonarchy. From France, Presbyterian polity then spread to the Netherlands, where the tradition of republican city governments made it a good fit for the churches. And then it went to Scotland, where the lairds had historically been in a constant struggle for power against the king. The lairds controlled the presbyteries—representative assemblies from churches in a relatively small geographic region—and used them to counterbalance the power of the king.[5]

However, none of this means that Calvin himself saw republicanism as essential for proper government. People could establish a covenant with a king, for example, and that would be perfectly appropriate. Less well known is the fact that when

5. For a detailed discussion of the origins of presbyterial polity, see my book *Reforming French Protestantism: The Development of Huguenot Ecclesiastical Institutions, 1557-1572*, Sixteenth Century Essays and Studies 66 (Kirksville, Missouri: Truman State University Press, 2003).

Calvin corresponded with the king of Poland about church government, he advised the use of bishops, a practice that is still followed in the Hungarian Reformed Church. It is also worth noting that, like the other major reformers, Calvin was a social conservative; he was opposed to revolutionary change. He thus never anticipated how his followers would later adapt his covenantal theory to support revolt and tyrannicide.

Historians frequently refer to Calvin's ideas as a *contract theory*. This is a bit of a misnomer. It would be far more accurate to refer to it as a *covenant theory*, and reserve *contract theory* for later, more secularized versions of Calvin's thought. Given that contract theory has become accustomed usage, it is too late to change it, but it is nonetheless important to remember its biblical roots in the idea of covenant.

VOLUNTARISTIC CHURCHES

The existence of state churches (or, for that matter, the Catholic system that preceded them), raised an important question: if you were born a citizen of the state, should you also be considered a member of the church? For nearly all sixteenth-century Europeans, the answer was obvious: yes, of course you should be. You were born into a family of church members, and your birth was marked by baptism, whereby you received your name. Why wouldn't you be a church member?

The idea that everyone needed a conversion experience to be a true Christian was not part of most Protestant thought. While conversion from Catholicism, for example, was recognized, a conversion experience was not considered essential for those who grew up in a church where the gospel was rightly preached and the sacraments were rightly administered.

Not everyone agreed with this way of thinking about church membership, however. Some radical reformers, such as Zwingli's opponent Conrad Grebel, the founder of the Swiss Brethren, believed that since the Bible described the church as the pure and spotless bride of Christ, admitting anyone and everyone into it was simply wrong: people who were not living a pure and holy life would sully the spotless bride, defiling her, and thus such people did not belong in the church. Rather, Grebel argued that there should be high membership standards, proving you were worthy, to get into the church and high standards to maintain membership. For those who didn't behave in ways approved by the group, harsh disciplinary practices such as shunning (having no contact with the person, also known as the ban) should be used to lead them to repentance.[6]

One implication of this understanding of church membership is that joining the church had to be a voluntary act, backed up by an appropriately holy life. This meant that children were not part of the church and thus could not be legitimately baptized. Grebel thus rebaptized adults who wished to join his church—he would say he baptized them properly for the first time—earning the group the derisive name *Anabaptists*, or *rebaptizers*. As often happens, the name which was originally intended as an insult was adopted by those following Grebel's ecclesiology as a badge of honor.

6. Using sociologist of religion Ernst Troeltsch's (1865–1923) typology of religious groups, this is a textbook example of a sect.

Conversion was not a necessary part of Anabaptist soteriology. What mattered was not having an experience, but the person's ongoing quality of life. That alone would determine if a person belonged in the church.

A second implication of Anabaptist ecclesiology is a changed relationship with the state. Twentieth-century historian and theologian George Huntston Williams distinguished two main branches of the Protestant Reformation: The mainstream reformers such as Luther and Calvin were *magisterial* reformers because they sought to work with the magistrate, that is, the government, in establishing their churches. The *radical* reformers, such as the Anabaptists, ostensibly had a sharp distinction between church and state and thus did not want the government to be involved with their churches.[7]

The heart of Anabaptist ecclesiology was the idea that the visible church had to conform as closely as possible to the invisible church. Mainstream reformers countered with Jesus's parable of the wheat and the weeds. In the parable, when the wheat and the weeds grow side by side, the owner of the land tells his servants not to pull the weeds so as not to pull out the wheat with them. He tells them instead to let them alone until harvest when they will be separated. Jesus then explains that the harvest is the end of the world and the harvesters are the

---

7. This distinction does not hold consistently. For example, when revolutionary Anabaptists (Williams's term) took over the city of Münster, they established their own government. This suggests that for some, the real difference was not whether they wanted a state church, but whether they could actually take over the state to establish their church.

angels. The point, according to the mainstream reformers, is that you cannot separate true and false believers in this world; that has to wait to the final judgment since we cannot see what is truly in a person's heart. Thus, the Anabaptist attempt to create a pure church in this world is doomed to failure.

Ultimately, by rejecting a critical rite of passage in society, the Anabaptists proved sufficiently disruptive that the mainstream reformers began persecuting and even executing them. They justified this by dusting off Constantine's anti-Donatist edict that made rebaptism—a typically Donatist act—a capital offense (see chapter 2). Since pretty much everyone in Zurich, where the Swiss Brethren began, had been baptized as infants, joining an Anabaptist church required rebaptism, which gave the authorities the excuse to attack them. Many were executed by giving them a "third baptism"—in other words, by drowning.

The Swiss Brethren scattered, and other Anabaptist groups arose in other areas. In the end, they had the last laugh: the voluntarist concept of the church that they promoted, minus some of their more extreme ecclesiology, became the norm throughout Europe and America, in large measure because of the rise of the secular state.

THE CHURCH AND THE SECULAR STATE

With the rise of secular states in the eighteenth and especially the nineteenth centuries, the cozy, covenantal relationship between church and state suggested by Two Kingdoms doctrine became less and less tenable, though most Lutheran churches still held to it. (State churches still exist in many primarily Lutheran countries.)

In place of Two Kingdoms doctrine, Reformed theologians such as Abraham Kuyper in the late nineteenth century and H. Richard Niebuhr in the twentieth suggested a Transformational model for the relationship of church and culture, where the church works to transform society (and with it, government) into progressively more godly forms. These thinkers drew inspiration from earlier models of social reform such as the British abolitionists, but they developed their own distinctive way of looking at the issue. The Transformationalist view is now the most common view among conservative Reformed Christians, so much so that it is often incorrectly assumed to have been Calvin's view. The misunderstanding is understandable: Calvin and his followers were certainly concerned with producing a godly society, and they expected the magistrate to carry out his God-given duties to promote the good and oppose evil. But Calvin's focus was always on the gospel, not on the kind of social action advocated in the Transformationalist model. According to Calvin, once the gospel was proclaimed and a true church established, we could work to make a godly society, but until that happened, activism in rooting out evils in society would amount to emphasizing the wrong things and, worse, could lead you to miss the gospel altogether.

IMPLICATIONS

The Protestant Reformation was a watershed event in European history that transformed many elements of European culture. In the realm of politics, and particularly in church-state relations, it had complex legacy. For our purposes, we need to revisit Two Kingdoms doctrine in light of the changing relationship between church and state since the Reformation.

Two Kingdoms doctrine was closely connected to the emerging Protestant state churches. In Luther's case, the church was subservient in most respects to the state, though neither could interfere with freedom of conscience. In Geneva, the church was a branch of the state, but maintained a higher degree of autonomy than did the church in Lutheran areas. But with the spread of religious liberty, the decline or elimination of state churches, and the adoption of a voluntaristic vision of the church that had more in common with the Anabaptists than with the mainstream Reformers, the close relationship between church and state was broken. Under these circumstances, the question became whether it was even possible to maintain Two Kingdoms doctrine.

The more radical Two Kingdoms advocates in the Reformed world see a sharp disjunction between the role of the church and the role of the state. The church's job is to proclaim the gospel; it is to have nothing to do with the civil sphere, whether in the form of entanglements with the state or in shaping and influencing culture. They claim that this was Calvin's view, but it is not that simple: Calvin clearly saw the church as an equal player with the state in the promotion of public morality, for example, and thus as being vitally involved with cultural transformation. At the same time, there is a grain of truth in the Reformed Two Kingdom view: as we have seen, Calvin did see preaching the gospel as the primary role of the church and sought to insulate both church and state from illicit interference from the other.

On the whole, however, in an environment in which the civil magistrate has no professional connections to the church, it is not at all clear that Two Kingdoms doctrine presents a coherent picture of church-state relations. The role of the state in promoting righteousness without imposing religion is good as far as it goes: It gives us a standard with which to evaluate government. So on a large scale, the conceptual model of the Two Kingdoms makes some sense. But there is no clear way to implement it, and it leaves no room for the church to speak out about the pressing issues of the day.

Calvin was right: the church's primary responsibility is to proclaim the kingdom, that is, the rule of Christ over all things. But that does not mean that the church cannot work in society to implement the *shalom* of God's Kingdom in our communities. Jesus and Paul both tell us that loving our neighbor as ourselves is the essence of God's *torah*, His instructions to us on how we are to live. If we believe that God's ways are the best for society, then out of love for our neighbor we should work to put His ways into practice in our communities. This means cultural engagement, not simply as consumers or even as critics, but as culture creators, bringing the values of the kingdom into the world around us.

To put it differently, the Transformationalist model discussed above captures much of what it means to be a believer in our cultural moment.

That does, of course, also mean engagement with politics, whether by voting, or lobbying, or running for office. Even with the American separation of church and state, we are not excused from seeking the good of our neighbor and of the city where God has sent us. And that means defending our neighbor's rights as we defend our own; resisting social, political, and economic chaos; and fighting Leviathan whenever government is guilty of overreach and trampling our liberties. But we'll discuss that in more detail later.

Thus far, our all-too-compressed overview of the relationship between church and state has left out one crucial question: what should we do if or when the state becomes hostile to Christianity? What do we do when the state commands us to do something that violates our conscience or tells us not to do something Christ obligates us to do? To put it differently, when does a legitimate government lose its legitimacy? When does a lawful king become an unlawful tyrant? And how are we to respond when that happen? We will explore these questions in the next chapters.

CHAPTER 6
PROTESTANT RESISTANCE THEORY

When we speak of all the people [resisting illegal commands of the king], we understand by that only those who hold their authority from the people, to wit, the magistrates, who are inferior to the king and whom the people have substituted or established, as it were, consorts in the empire, and with a kind of tribunitial authority to restrain the encroachments of the sovereignty, and to represent the whole body of the people. —STEPHEN JUNIUS BRUTUS, *VINDICIAE CONTRA TYRANNOS* (1579)

In the previous chapter, we looked at the foundations of Protestant political thought in the sixteenth century, notably Luther's doctrine of the Two Kingdoms. The right-hand kingdom consists of the true church, which is invisible and known only to God; the left-hand kingdom is in the visible world and is governed under God via the state and the church. Since the state is ordained by God, Christians need to acknowledge and follow its authority.

But what happens when the state turns against God? What do we do if it orders us to do something that God forbids or forbids something that God commands? Do we have a right to resist? Is there a right to self-defense against the government?

LUTHER IN THE 1520S

Luther's relationship with the law was complicated. He was excommunicated in 1520 and declared an imperial outlaw by Holy Roman Emperor Charles V in 1521, which meant it was open season on him: he could be killed on sight by anyone who found him. Fortunately, Luther's patron, Frederick the Wise, elector of Saxony, hid him away for a time at the Wartburg, a castle outside of Eisenach, and then protected him when he returned to Wittenberg.

In the Knights' Revolt of 1522, a group of knights led by Franz von Sickingen and Ulrich von Hutten decided to try to take over Trier, a city headed by its archbishop who was also one of the electors of the Holy Roman emperor. There were both political and religious reasons for the attack. The knights had become increasingly irrelevant in the Holy Roman Empire and were not even represented in the Diet (the Imperial parliament). Further, von Sickingen and von Hutten were supporters of Protestantism, so when Luther was excommunicated and declared an outlaw, they declared a vendetta against the Catholic Church. Since Trier was run by its archbishop and was the weakest of the electors, it looked like a good choice.

Unfortunately for von Sickingen, the archbishop proved to be a much more capable soldier than expected. He led a spirited defense of the city, and when a relief army arrived, von Sickingen was forced to withdraw. He was soon captured after a brief siege of one of his castles, which was largely destroyed by the gunpowder artillery deployed against him. Von Sickingen was severely wounded and died of his injuries shortly after his capture.

Von Sickingen's ally, Ulrich von Hutten, fled to Switzerland, where he met briefly with Zwingli. He then withdrew to a monastery and died shortly thereafter as one of the first European victims of syphilis.

Luther responded to the Knights' Revolt with his treatise *On Secular Authority* (1523). In this work, he spells out the Two Kingdoms doctrine discussed in the last chapter and explains the Christian's relationship with secular law. Citizens of the right-hand kingdom—true Christians—have no need for law and are free to act according to the dictates of love. However, given that there are relatively few Christians in the world, law is necessary for society to function. Thus, Christians ought to obey the law out of love of neighbor just as they obey God's law out of love for him. And since law and government are necessary, Christians are free to work in government even, say, as an executioner out of love of neighbor. This is an implicit condemnation of actions like the

Knights' Revolt since it was a rebellion against duly constituted government.

That said, however, Luther also argued that neither church
nor state has the right to bind consciences. This means that
the state should not be involved in prosecuting heresy, for example. If the Word of God properly preached cannot correct
heresy, no amount of government coercion can.

This stance in support of secular authority except in matters
of conscience was, if anything, strengthened by the German
Peasants' War (1524–25). The Peasants' War was triggered by
a combination of economic stress, increased demands by nobles on the peasants, and radical preaching by men such as
Thomas Müntzer, who saw himself as a new Elijah sent to
free the peasants from their spiritual and physical bondage.
Hundreds of thousands of peasants, supported by Anabaptist
preachers and radical spiritualists such as Müntzer, rose up
across Germany, rioting and attacking the wealthy, the nobles, and monasteries.

At great personal risk, Luther traveled from Saxony to the
neighboring territory of Thuringia to try to mediate the dispute. His initial attitude was that the peasants were insolent
and should not have revolted but that they had legitimate
grievances that were the fault of the nobility. He urged a
peaceful resolution of the conflict. But in the face of the violence he saw in Thuringia, he hurried back to Wittenberg
where he penned one of his most notorious works, a tract
called *Against the Murdering, Thieving Hordes of Peasants*.[1] He

1. The original title was *Against the Rioting Peasants*, but printers changed it
without Luther's consent.

argued in this that there was nothing more poisonous than a rebel, and that the nobles should put down the peasants like mad dogs, using every weapon in their arsenal to do so.

The nobles complied.

A combined Lutheran and Catholic army led by the young Lutheran nobleman Philip of Hesse met the peasants near a town called Frankenhausen and slaughtered somewhere between one and three thousand of them in a one-sided rout that hardly deserves the name battle.

Luther later defended his words, though he condemned the nobles for the excessive slaughter at Frankenhausen and said they would be judged by God for it.

Through the 1520s, Luther remained consistent in his attitude toward civil authority. Following Romans 13:1–7, he argued that since government is established by God, we are to obey it unless it commands us to do something contrary to God's Law or prohibits us from doing something God commands. By the 1530s, however, conditions on the ground would force Luther to reconsider and modify his thinking on the matter.

THE BEGINNING OF PROTESTANT RESISTANCE THEORY

Holy Roman Emperor Charles V was interested in church reform, but he was a dedicated Catholic who did not want Protestantism in his Empire (or anywhere else, for that matter). He thus opposed the spread of Lutheran ideas, but during the 1520s and '30s he could do little about it. He was faced with external threats from France and the expanding

Ottoman Empire and even fought a war with the pope. He could not afford internal conflict within the Holy Roman Empire as well. He verbally opposed Protestantism but was unable to do anything effective against its spread.

Meanwhile, numerous cities and territories in the Empire were adopting Protestant ideas. Given the Emperor's opposition to Protestantism, they knew it was only a matter of time before he acted against them. To prevent him from picking off the Protestant territories one at a time, they decided to form a defensive alliance: should the Emperor attack one of them, they would consider it an attack on all of them. Before the alliance was formalized, they asked for Luther's blessing on the project.

He refused.

Luther argued on the basis of Romans 13 that we are to obey all governing powers and, therefore, that the princes needed to obey the emperor. If he asked them to do something they could not do in good conscience, if he asked them to do something God prohibited or not to do something God commanded, then their only choice would be civil disobedience—obeying God and conscience and accepting the consequences. Only by doing so could we honor the God-given authority of the emperor.

It is worth noting that Luther was not following his own advice consistently at this point. He had been declared an imperial outlaw, and anyone harboring him was guilty of a crime against the empire. Luther could justify flight and hiding on the basis of his unalienable right to life (as noted in chapter 4), but Elector Frederick should not have protected Luther or allowed him to live and teach openly in Wittenberg. Yet somehow, he did not admonish Frederick on this point.

In his response to the proposed alliance, Luther was undoubtedly reacting to the Knights' Revolt and the German Peasants' War—he was a social conservative who opposed anything that looked like revolt or rebellion. The bloody results of the Peasants' War in particular gave Luther a real fear of social uprisings, and as a result, he condemned all forms of rebellion against duly constituted governments.

This was not the answer the princes wanted. They needed Luther's approval, so they did the only logical thing they could think of: they sent in the lawyers.

The lawyers told Luther that what he said about Romans 13 was true in most circumstances and for most people, but it did not apply to the princes in the empire. First, the princes were themselves governing authorities. They were part of the powers that be that we were told to obey. Paul did not write Romans with princes in mind, but common people who had no part in government and who were to obey those put in authority over them by God. Luther's response was that God had placed the emperor over the princes, so it was their duty to obey him. Not so fast, said the lawyers. The emperor was elected by seven electors who represented the princes of the empire. Since they elect the emperor, they have not only the right but the duty to oversee him in accordance with the constitution of the empire. Should the emperor violate the law or break his word, it was not just their right to resist him; it was their legal responsibility to do so.

RESISTANCE BY THE LESSER MAGISTRATES

Luther listened to the arguments and was persuaded. In 1530, he issued the Torgau memorandum, in which he said that if the lawyers were correct about the constitution of the empire, in other words, if the princes were responsible under the law to lead resistance against the emperor should he break his word or violate the law, then it was also theologically acceptable for them to do so. The common person had no right of rebellion—the Peasants' War was unjustifiable—but if resistance were led by "lesser magistrates" (also called "inferior magistrates"), it was legitimate at least within the context of the Holy Roman Empire.

The Torgau memorandum provided the theological justification for the Schmalkaldic League, a Protestant alliance, which was founded the next year. The subsequent history of the league is not particularly important for our purposes; the key here is that the memorandum laid the foundation for the subsequent development of Protestant resistance theory and particularly the idea that only resistance led by lesser magistrates was legitimate.

As in so many other areas, Luther's thinking on resistance theory was widely adopted by other Protestant leaders. Among the leading continental reformers, John Calvin and Peter Martyr Vermigli both followed Luther's lead, though they generalized the idea of resistance led by the lesser magistrate to all states, not just the Holy Roman Empire. Others took the argument considerably further, particularly the Marian Exiles (Protestant refugees who fled into exile when the Catholic Mary Stuart became queen of England). We will examine that in the next chapter. Here, we turn to the next major developments in continental Protestant resistance theory.

THE FRENCH WARS OF RELIGION

In France in the sixteenth century, religious conflict tore apart the kingdom. The Catholic Church was deeply intertwined with all aspects of French life, so much so that any attempt to reform French society inevitably involved reform of the church. And the French church was ripe for reform. Popular Catholicism was shot through with superstition and an obsession with seeing portents of the end of the world and the coming of the antichrist. And as was true elsewhere in Europe, the upper clergy were more politicians than religious leaders, though some of them did try to improve the spiritual state of their dioceses.

When the Reformation hit, however, the Sorbonne—the theological faculty of the University of Paris—began holding heresy trials. King Francis I blew hot and cold on reform at first, allowing some trials but shutting others down when they got too close to the royal family. This did not last, however. He cracked down on Protestants in 1534 when placards attacking the Catholic Mass and transubstantiation appeared across France and even reportedly on the door of the royal bedchamber in his chateau in Amboise. Persecution would continue to varying degrees for most of the rest of the century.

Despite Francis's persecution, religious reform continued at a grassroots level and among some key intellectual leaders. Up to the 1540s, this reform was a messy, wide-ranging affair with Catholic reformers influenced by Renaissance humanism, every variety of Protestantism imaginable, and even ideas that both Catholics and mainstream Protestants would have considered heretical. This began to change in the 1540s when Calvin started publishing high-quality theological works in French. No one had done this before, and Calvin's highly rational approach to theology provided an escape from the superstition and angst of popular French Catholicism.

These writings hit right about the time that increasing numbers of the French nobility and even princes of the blood (i.e., members of the royal family) were converting to Protestantism. The more rational approach to religion taken by Calvin was probably a factor in this, but in general, the conversions seem more influenced by social networks than by theology. When one person converted, it was likely that other members of the family as well as patrons and clients would also convert.

Once the nobility began adopting Protestant ideas, the situation in France became considerably more volatile. Catholic attacks on Huguenot (French Protestant) services led the Huguenots to arm themselves; in retaliation, Catholic churches were vandalized. And the Huguenot nobility had military forces at their disposal, raising the specter of civil war. The power behind the throne was the queen mother, Catherine de Medici, who was determined to find a way to stabilize France to secure her son's position. Her chancellor, Michel de l'Hôpital, negotiated a decree known as the Edict of January (1562), which allowed Protestant worship outside of cities and in the town houses of the Protestant nobility.

The Catholic law courts refused to recognize the edict. Then the ultra-Catholic Guise family found a Protestant congregation worshipping in a barn outside of a town called Vassy. Even though they were worshipping legally by the terms of the edict, Guise's men attacked them, killing sixty-three and wounding a hundred more. When word spread, other massacres followed.

The Huguenots responded by mobilizing their armies at Orléans and taking several towns along the Loire Valley. The king mobilized his troops and thus began the first of an interminable series of Wars of Religion in France. They followed a standard pattern: there would be a provocation (often by the Guises), a war would break out, the two sides would fight to exhaustion, a truce would be declared with the Huguenots receiving either more or fewer rights to worship depending on the results on the battlefield, and the truce would hold until another provocation triggered the next war. Rinse and repeat.

This was exactly what Catherine de Medici was trying to avoid. She decided to try a diplomatic solution: she proposed that she marry her daughter Marguerite to Henri de Bourbon, King of Navarre, Prince of the Blood, and the highest-born leader on the Protestant side. The Huguenots accepted, and they were guaranteed safe conduct to Paris for the wedding.

THE SAINT BARTHOLOMEW'S DAY MASSACRES

The king by this time was Charles IX, a weak-willed man who during the truce increasingly fell under the influence of Gaspard de Coligny, another Huguenot Prince of the Blood, the admiral of France, and the real political leader of the Huguenot side. The Guises hated Coligny, and so after the wedding but during the safe conduct, they hired an assassin to kill him. The assassin failed; Coligny was severely wounded but did not die. The Huguenots were outraged, and the royal council panicked: they convinced themselves that the Huguenots were going to seek revenge by killing the royal family. They decided to finish off Coligny and tell everyone that he was plotting against the king, but that no other Huguenots were involved and that the safe conduct would continue to be honored. Unfortunately, when Henri de Guise was sent to kill Coligny, the instructions got garbled, and the town guard began a massacre of all the Protestants in the city on St. Bartholomew's Day, August 23, 1572. When word spread, copycat massacres followed across France. Estimates of the death toll range from five thousand to thirty thousand.[2]

Although the massacre seems to have been unplanned, King Charles IX took responsibility and claimed (falsely)

---

2. There are a variety of interpretations of exactly what happened on St. Bartholomew's Day. This is the most likely explanation. See Barbara Diefendorf, *Beneath the Cross: Catholics and Huguenots in Sixteenth-Century Paris* (Oxford, 1991).

that those killed in Paris had been conspiring against him. The conspirators were dead, he said, so Huguenots were free to return safely to their homes.

The St. Bartholomew's Day massacres had a range of effects. They triggered another War of Religion, of course. Catholics who were disgusted by the slaughter formed a new faction known as the *Politiques* because they were dedicated to finding a political solution to the religious conflict in France. On the Protestant side, many Huguenots returned to Catholicism: if Protestantism were the true church, why did God allow them to get slaughtered?

Not all did, however, and that raised two additional problems. First, the older, experienced, and more diplomatically inclined leaders were all killed in Paris, leaving the leadership of the movement in the hands of younger, more hotheaded men. Second, up to this point, the Huguenots had argued that they were loyal to the king but opposed his evil advisors who were misleading him about the Protestants. Now they were faced with a king who claimed responsibility for the slaughter of thousands of their coreligionists.

THE MONARCHOMACHS

As far as the Huguenots were concerned, a king who murders his own people has beyond question turned into a tyrant. The question was how to respond. Three key works were written during this period by a group of writers that became known as the Monarchomachs. The first, François Hotman's *Francogallia*, was published in Geneva in 1573.

This work was begun well before the St. Bartholomew's Day massacres as an argument against the growing absolutism of the French court. A product of an era that believed that the true nature of anything was found in its origins, Hotman argues that France's king was originally an elected chief magistrate who ruled in conjunction with the other estates in an essentially Aristotelian mixed state. The government was thus fundamentally republican, and this only changed when Roman lawyers corrupted the system. In its origins, Hotman argues, France was a commonwealth built on consent of the governed and established through covenant. To reform French society it was necessary to return it to its original pristine state, and this in turn justified general resistance to monarchial overreach and tyranny.

The second work, written by Calvin's protégé Theodore Beza, was *Du droit des magistrats* (1574). In this work, Beza argues (similarly to Hotman) that monarchy was originally elective. He supports this by citing biblical passages that show that the people of Israel ratified Saul and David as their kings. He further points out that "the people" existed before the king, and thus that the king obtained his power from them. Beza follows Calvin in arguing that, at their root, governments are covenantal and based on the consent of the governed. Since it is illogical that this grant of power would be unconditional, the people do have a right to resist unjust rule. All people, without exception, have not only the right but the responsibility to oppose usurpers. Against legitimate kings turned tyrants, Beza follows Luther and Calvin in arguing for resistance led by the lesser magistrate.

The third work was *Vindiciae contra tyrannos* (1579), written under the pseudonym Stephen Junius Brutus.[3] The *Vindiciae* focuses its argument on the tension between obedience to God and obedience to the government. The core of its argument is that government exists as a twofold covenant. The first covenant involves God on one side and the people and the king on the other, in which the people and king agree to obey God. In the second, between the king and the people, the people agree to obey the king as long as he rules justly. Should the king violate either of these covenants, the people have a right and duty to resist him. The *Vindiciae* stops short of arguing for a general right of rebellion, however: it continues to argue for resistance led by the lesser magistrate, in keeping with the mainstream Protestant tradition.

The *Vindiciae* would influence John Locke's political thought and was cited by John Adams as an important argument for liberty. Its conclusions, however, were reasonably conventional for continental Protestant resistance theory: it took a socially conservative position to avoid popular uprisings, instead relying on existing elites in government to lead resistance when necessary. Perhaps the reason for this was that there were nobles and princes of the blood willing and able to oppose the monarchy in the name of Protestantism. In Britain, resistance theory would take a more radical turn.

3. The most likely candidates for authorship are Philippe de Mornay, Hubert Languet, or perhaps both. See *Vindiciae contra Tyrannos: A Defense of Liberty against Tyrants*, translated by William Walker, introduction by Glenn Sunshine (Canon Press, 2020).

IMPLICATIONS

The mainstream Protestant Reformers were all social conservatives. They feared the violence and chaos that could easily be unleashed by religious radicals in their day, and thus they insisted that reform be done in an orderly manner with the support and under the direction of the magistrate. But they needed to find a way to respond to the threat of wars of extermination aimed at them by Charles V and the Valois kings of France. The unalienable right to life and the resulting right—even obligation—of self-defense led quite naturally to the idea of banding together to protect their lives and the Reformation. But how far can you go with this? How do you prevent this from degenerating into social chaos and vendetta? The answer was to insist that resistance be led by the lesser magistrates, that is, by men in lower offices of the government. That way, those in resistance would still be able to honor the political leaders God placed over them and avoid the anarchy of the German Peasants' War.

Like the Reformers, we need to reject violence, rioting, looting, anarchy, and chaos in the name of social change. No matter how good the cause, these actions are never justified. We must not go as far as Luther and call upon the magistrate to slaughter the rioters, but we do need to support and encourage efforts to restore calm.

But what about attacks on us and on our liberty?

First, we live in a different political environment than the Reformers. In a republic, we have more options to respond to threats than they did five hundred years ago, and we should make use of them.

Second, the Reformers did not take action until they were threatened with war. Persecution, heresy trials, even brutal executions, did not trigger a violent response for self-defense. Some died; others, like Calvin, fled into exile. But they did not take up arms until it became necessary to defend the larger community against the attacks of Catholic forces, whether led by the Habsburgs, the Valois, or the Guises.

In other words, violent resistance was only triggered when it was needed to defend the community—out of love of neighbor, not love of self.

Further, these acts of violent resistance were done in accord with traditional just war theory. They were acts of self-defense led by legitimate members of the government rather than private citizens. The insistence on the lesser magistrate thus avoided not only the problem of anarchy and insurrection, but affirmed the teaching in Romans 13 about the role of governing authorities and our relationship to them, and fit at least loosely the accepted tenets of just war theory.

CHAPTER 7
RESISTANCE THEORY IN BRITAIN

I put for the general inclination of all mankind, a perpetual and restless desire of power after power, that ceaseth only in death.

—THOMAS HOBBES (1588-1679)

In the last chapter, we looked at continental Protestant Resistance Theory. The consensus, beginning with Luther's Torgau memorandum (1530), was that when the king broke the fundamental laws of God or of the kingdom, the lesser magistrates had the right and responsibility to lead resistance against the king.

In Britain, resistance theory went in a more radical direction. England had broken with Rome under Henry VIII, though it is an exaggeration to say at this point that it had

113

become Protestant. His successor, Edward VI, worked to make England fully Protestant with the support and direction of Thomas Cranmer, the archbishop of Canterbury. When Edward died young in 1553, he was succeeded by his half-sister, Mary I. Mary Tudor was a reactionary Catholic: she rejected reforms introduced into the church by the Council of Trent, she refused to allow the Jesuits into the kingdom, and she began to persecute Protestants systematically, having any she caught burned alive in the public square. Her most notable victim was Archbishop Cranmer himself.

THE MARIAN EXILES

Mary's persecutions led hundreds of English Protestants to flee the kingdom, primarily for Reformed areas in the Rhineland, Switzerland, and Geneva (which was not yet part of the Swiss Confederation). Many received theological training, and all deeply imbibed Reformed theology. Some of the exiles wrote political and theological treatises addressing the situation back in England. Two of the most important of these were John Poynet and Christopher Goodman.

Poynet was a prominent Protestant leader in Edward VI's England. By 1545, he had become the chaplain of Thomas Cranmer, the archbishop of Canterbury. In 1550, he became bishop of Rochester, and in 1551 was named bishop of Winchester. But upon the ascent of Mary Tudor to the throne in 1553, Poynet and his wife fled England for the continent. (Even though clerical marriage had not yet been made legal, he married in 1548.) Poynet's exact movements during this period are not known, but in 1556 he published his key work on political theology, *A Shorte Treatise of Politike Power*. This treatise, which would influence John Locke and American Founders such as John Adams, explored the question of when a legitimate monarch turned into an illegitimate tyrant, a core question that other Protestants would need to address during the era of the Wars of Religion. Poynet's arguments were based on Peter Martyr Vermigli's work, and, like Vermigli, Poynet emphasized the role of the lesser magistrate in resisting an unjust ruler. Unlike Vermigli, however, Poynet argued in favor of tyrannicide, a considerably more radical position than earlier Protestants had taken.

Goodman, who according to some sources held the Lady Margaret professorship of divinity at Oxford, left England in 1554 and made his way to Geneva via Strasbourg and Frankfurt. He and John Knox were both made pastors in Geneva in 1555. The two were quite a pair. In 1558, Knox published his notorious *First Blast of the Trumpet against the Monstrous Regiment of Women*—an attack on women monarchs in the era of Mary Queen of Scots, Mary Tudor, and Catherine de Medici, three women who were viewed as being behind persecution of Protestants. That same year, Goodman published *How Superior Powers Ought to Be Obeyed by Their Subjects, and Wherein They May Lawfully by God's Word Be Disobeyed and Resisted*.

The irony of this is that later that year, Mary died, and her younger half-sister, Elizabeth I, ascended the English throne. Despite their apologies, she never forgave either Knox or Goodman, and so on their return they worked on religious reform in Scotland rather than England.

Goodman's treatise argued that although it would be best if resistance to tyranny were led by the lesser magistrates, if lower officials failed to take that responsibility, the common people could rise against the tyrant. Further, Romans 13 only applies to legitimate kings who reward good and punish evil, as the text itself shows; it does not apply to tyrants who punish good and reward evil. In fact, since tyranny comes from Satan, to obey a tyrant is to rebel against God. Far from being a sin, resistance to tyranny is therefore an obligation in the sight of God. Both of these points—resistance by the people if the lesser magistrate refused to act, and resistance to tyranny as a requirement before God—were far more radical positions than any Protestant leader (except perhaps Thomas Müntzer and his Anabaptist ilk) had yet taken. It was even more radical than the position taken by the Monarchomachs in France in the wake of the St. Bartholomew's Day massacres that would take place two decades later.

COVENANT VERSUS DIVINE RIGHT

At the heart of both Poynet's and Goodman's treatises was a covenantal view of government derived from Reformed and, specifically, Calvinist thought: all authority derives from God, who delegates His authority to the people; they in turn delegate their authority to the king to execute true justice, in line with God's will, on behalf of the people. If the king ever saw himself as an absolute monarch and acted against God and the people, they had the right to revoke the authority delegated to him and to rebel, particularly if they were led by inferior magistrates who were themselves part of the government as established by God.

In contrast, royalists across Europe, including Britain, adopted a more absolutist vision of the state, arguing instead for the divine right of kings: monarchs were appointed directly by God as a kind of mediator between God and the people. The king's laws were to be obeyed as if they were God's laws. If the king ordered something contrary to divine law, the people were nonetheless obligated to obey the king, and the king alone would answer for his errors. According to absolutists, there can never be grounds for resisting royal authority: The king speaks for God, and if he gets it wrong, the people will be held guiltless if they "sin" by obeying him.

This was a new development in political theory: as we have seen, in the Middle Ages, government was always limited, and no one was trusted with the kind of absolute power the divine right of kings advocated. But medieval theorists did not have to deal with religious conflict on the scale of the Wars of Religion. Divine right advocates believed that the only way to prevent such wars was to equate obedience to the king with obedience to God. This negated religion as a potentially revolutionary force in society, contradicting the covenantal views of government and by Protestant resistance theory.

GEORGE BUCHANAN AND SAMUEL RUTHERFORD

The divine right of kings prompted a strong reaction among English and Scottish theologians, who based their arguments against it largely on Calvinist social contract theory. The most radical was Scottish thinker George Buchanan. Buchanan's *De jure regni apud Scotos* (1579) started with standard Calvinist covenantal thinking but pushed its implications far beyond continental thinking. Buchanan argued that power resided in the people, who delegated it to the king, but only conditionally. The king was bound by the conditions placed on him when he came to power and so was not above the law: if he broke the law, he should be punished like any other person; if he violated the terms of the contract that gave him power, he became a common outlaw. While Buchanan expected the lairds (the Scottish nobility) to lead in resistance to outlaw kings as they had so often done in the past, he also allowed private individuals to take up arms against the king if need be, just as they could against any other outlaw. This echoed the argument made by Goodman that private citizens had a right to rebel if the lesser magistrate failed to act; it also implied support for Poynet's argument for tyrannicide. But the idea of treating the king as an outlaw was a bridge too far for many. The book was condemned by Parliament in 1584 and again in 1664, and Oxford University burned it in 1683.

More typical was another Scottish theologian, Samuel Rutherford. His *Lex, Rex, or the Law and the Prince* (1644) argues once again the standard covenantal view that power comes from God to the people, who then delegate it to governments. Government is established by a covenant built on a moral framework drawn from natural law, which he identifies with divine law. He comments, "What is warranted by the direction of nature's light is warranted by the law of nature, and consequently by a divine law; for who can deny the law of nature to be a divine law?"[1] Natural law and divine law also are the basis of biblical law and should inform positive law (i.e., human legislation).

Rutherford explains that there are a variety of legitimate forms of government, but in all cases, authority is vested in offices, not in the persons who hold those offices. Thus, in a monarchy, the office of the king has authority, not the person of the king himself. This means that it is possible to depose the king without undermining royal authority. In order to break the covenant established with the government, the people need a just cause rooted in a violation of natural law; one of the duties of preachers in these circumstances is to explain carefully the moral case for or against resistance to the government. Unlike Buchanan, Rutherford argues that when resistance is justified, it must be led by the lesser magistrates. The people have no direct right of rebellion, though he does note the example of the people saving Jonathan from Saul in 1 Samuel 14:45.

RADICALS IN THE ENGLISH CIVIL WAR

Lex, Rex was written in the early days of the English Civil War. The details of the war are too complex to summarize here. Of greater significance for our purposes were the ideas of the more radical groups associated with the Parliamentarian side. Some of these were relatively small and did not have a systematic approach to government, basing their ideas instead on a

---

1. Samuel Rutherford, *Lex, Rex* (Moscow, ID: Canon Press, 2020), 13.

vision of what government or society should be. For example, Fifth Monarchists believed they were inaugurating the fifth kingdom of Daniel 2 that would be ruled by King Jesus; what this Fifth Monarchy would look like was less than clear but would presumably become evident when Jesus began to reign. Others had less of a theological than a social vision. For example, Diggers were radical egalitarians who believed people should live in small, self-sufficient rural communities with no social or political hierarchy and no private property.

The most significant of these radical groups was the Levelers, so named because they wanted to level out the social hierarchy. Unlike the Diggers, they accepted the idea of private property, and they had a far more coherent political program outlined in *An Agreement of the People*, a series of manifestos published from 1647 to 1649 that developed with the changing conditions in England during the Civil War. The basic demands were freedom of religion (later versions exclude Roman Catholicism from this), frequent convening of Parliament, and equality before the law. In its final form, the *Agreement* included provisions for equal representation in Parliament, suffrage of all adult male property holders, the right to remain silent in court, the right not to be drafted into the army, and a host of other rights that we recognize today. Although the influence of the Levelers in England waned after 1650, scholars believe that *An Agreement of the People* was a significant influence on the American Constitution.

Although the radicals were divided among themselves and from the mainstream Parliamentary side, they were all united in their belief that King Charles I had violated the rights of the people. English Calvinists anchored rights in natural law and further argued that idolatry was a violation of natural law and hence the rights of the people. Entrenched idolatry was thus legitimate grounds for rebellion against the king as a violation of the king's covenant with God and with the people. In this way, English Calvinism developed a truly explosive political ideology far more radical than the better-known ideas of John Locke, who was in many ways its successor. The irony is that Calvin himself likely would have repudiated this revolutionary interpretation of his political thought.

HOBBES AND THE DIVINE RIGHT OF KINGS

This thinking not only went against continental interpretations of covenantal government, it also naturally generated a response from supporters of the divine right of kings. The most important English theorist on this side is Thomas Hobbes. To understand Hobbes, we need to back up and look at larger philosophical debates from the Renaissance into the seventeenth century that at first glance seem to have nothing to do with politics.

MECHANICAL PHILOSOPHY

Although the Renaissance is frequently seen as the beginnings of modern science, it was more the Golden Age of magic theory. Renaissance thinkers such as Marsilio Ficino, Giovanni Pico della Mirandola, and Heinrich Cornelius Agrippa prepared learned treatises on magic, and the magus John Dee served

Elizabeth I's court. Magic was divided into two types, artificial magic and natural magic. Artificial magic was done using demons, the spirits of the dead, and the like; it was universally recognized as evil. Fortune-telling, whether done via spirits or via astrology, was also seen as evil since it was attempting to discover things God had hidden from us. Natural magic involved using "occult" (Latin for "hidden") forces that were built into the fabric of the universe by God. Many naturally occurring events were explained by these forces rather than by normal physical causes. Natural magicians studied these occult forces and could manipulate them to produce effects in this world. Since it was done through using natural forces, natural magic was, in principle, morally neutral, though given that the information about the occult forces might have been obtained from demons, it was always viewed with suspicion.

Growing rationalism in the seventeenth century led to a backlash against the entire idea of occult forces and natural magic. An alternative explanation of natural phenomena known as mechanical philosophy emerged that argued that everything in the physical world could be explained by mechanical interactions between particles—pushing, pulling, colliding, rubbing, etc. Prominent mechanical philosophers included René Descartes and . . . Thomas Hobbes.

LEVIATHAN

Hobbes was born in 1588. He was educated at Oxford and spent the years between 1630 and 1637 in Paris, where he adopted the ideas of mechanical philosophy. He returned to

England in 1637 and wrote a treatise on politics. His ideas proved to be unpopular, so he returned to Paris in 1640, where he stayed throughout the English Civil War. Among other things, during this period he became the tutor to the future Charles II, the son of Charles I, against both of whom the English Civil War was fought. Influenced by the royalist exiles in his circle, Hobbes also composed the work he is best remembered for, *Leviathan, or the Matter, Forme and Power of a Commonwealth, Ecclesiasticall and Civil* (completed 1650 but not published until 1651).

The title of *Leviathan* seems to have been chosen from what was believed to be its etymology: it was thought to come from the Hebrew *lavah*, meaning "to couple, connect, or join" and *thannin*, meaning "serpent or dragon." The creature was called leviathan either because its size made it hard to believe it was a single creature or because its scales were tightly pressed together. The image of the state on Hobbes's frontispiece was of a giant man holding a crozier (for ecclesiastical power) and a sword (for civil power), with a body made up of three hundred smaller men, all facing inward except one face looking outward. The state is thus depicted as a single entity made up of individuals bound together in an omnipotent, immortal, and indivisible whole under its head, the king.

Although it might not seem relevant, Hobbes's commitment to mechanical philosophy had important implications for his political theories. We see this almost immediately in Part I of his book, dealing with anthropology. He argues that human beings are purely material creatures, with no immaterial soul or mind.[2] All we are comes from mechanical interactions between the particles that make up our bodies. Contrary to other political philosophers, Hobbes argues that there is no *summum bonum* (highest good) to which humanity or the state can aspire. There is, however, a *summum malum* (highest evil) which we must avoid at all costs: the state of nature, which Hobbes sees as anarchy, a constant war of all against all, in which human life is "nasty, brutish, and short."

According to Hobbes, to deliver them from the state of nature, people establish government via a social contract—an emphatically secularized version of the covenant theory advocated in the Reformed tradition in which Hobbes had been educated. In this contract, people collectively give up their right of self-government to the civil government, whether a monarch or an assembly. (Hobbes reflects on Aristotle's three basic forms of government and states his clear preference for monarchy.) Once that contract is made, it is irrevocable, since one contract cannot override another. Further, the sovereign, by definition, cannot violate the covenant since the covenant grants all rights to him, nor can he commit injustice or violate the rights of the citizens since they have voluntarily given up their rights to the sovereign. The sovereign decides all matters of government and of religion, since to allow others to make those decisions is to invite discord of the sort seen

---

2. Hobbes's religious views have been subject to much debate. He was not an atheist but seems to have believed that God was the Creator and that He was in some sense part of the material world. It is probably best to think of him as a somewhat quirky Deist, given his recognition of God as Creator and his insistence on strict mechanical philosophy.

in the English Civil War. Even though he supports the idea of a Christian commonwealth and offers his own ideas about religion, Hobbes leaves decisions on religion in the hands of the sovereign.

Leviathan was thus an apt title of the book for reasons beyond etymology: it pointed to a totalizing vision of the state that was not only made up of all the people under the king, but whose reach extended into every area of life, even religion and conscience. Hobbes's anthropology, rooted as it was in mechanical philosophy and incipient materialism, had no room for abstract ideas such as unalienable, natural rights; everything was mechanical and empirical, and thus could and should be properly placed under state control in the name of preventing us from falling back into the chaos and anarchy of nature.

The book immediately generated strong reactions. The royalists in France, together with Anglicans and Catholics elsewhere, hated it for its rampant secularism. His life likely in danger, Hobbes fled back to London in 1651, submitted to the government there, and was allowed to live quietly in London. With the Restoration in 1660, his old pupil Charles was now king. Charles II granted Hobbes a small pension and, more importantly, a degree of protection. His views, often in distorted form, were widely denounced, and Parliament attempted to try him for heresy. This came to naught, but he was prohibited from publishing anything else related to human society or behavior.

Hobbes is important for our purposes for two things. First, he provides a counterpoint to resistance theory, arguing in essence that resistance against a duly constituted government is never legitimate and that kings cannot become tyrants since nothing that they do is subject to question. This of course comes from the assumption that there are no unalienable or natural rights that the king is obligated to recognize (materialistic mechanical philosophy again). Second, Hobbes secularizes covenantal politics into social contract theory. This demonstrates that even among monarchists, the idea of some sort of consent of the governed was recognized and understood in terms largely compatible with Reformed political thought. But Hobbes divorced it from its connection to God's covenant with us and the bilateral nature of the state's covenant with the people. By eliminating natural rights and mutual responsibilities between the sovereign and the people, Hobbes created an argument for absolutism and the divine right of kings. But he also converted covenantalism into contractualism, laying the groundwork for Locke and other later advocates of limited government, natural rights, and resistance theory expressed in contractual language divorced from its theological roots. Ironically, this aspect of *Leviathan* provided a conceptual framework for the theorists who would decisively end absolutism in England.

IMPLICATIONS

The English Civil War produced a backlash in Britain against religion both culturally and politically. On a cultural level, religious enthusiasm was frowned upon. Instead, the only acceptable religion was pro forma attendance at church and participation in the sacraments. The great irony of this is that, as we will see, this approach to Christianity only survived because the Methodists and British Evangelicals so infected the lower classes with enthusiasm that it kept England from following the French into a destructive anti-Christian revolution. In the short term, however, after the Restoration, dissent against the Church of England was suppressed, and dissenters were punished severely.

The English Civil War helped to change political theory in ways that still shape political discourse today. Up to that point, political theory was rooted in religion—Augustinianism, covenant, God-given rights, and so on. But the seventeenth century saw a reaction against the dominance of historic Christianity in intellectual and public life. The backlash against wars of religion together with the growth of rationalism and empiricism led to an increasingly secularized view of the world. In this context and especially as he worked with the son and heir of Charles I, it is not surprising that Hobbes would develop an explicitly secular vision of politics based on the rejection of the soul or other immaterial parts of the human person. As a result, his political system replaced covenant with contract, rejected any role for God in establishing the polity, and left questions of religion entirely up to the sovereign. Other continental thinkers were moving in a similar direction, but no major political theorist had gone so far so fast as Hobbes.

Even with growing secularization, the underlying culture of early modern Europe remained profoundly Christian. Concepts of right and wrong, for example, were rooted deeply in Christianity. And while Hobbes was at the head of an unstoppable trend toward secularizing political theory, Christian concepts surrounding unalienable rights and resistance to tyranny continued to play a major role among opponents of absolutism.

CHAPTER 8
LOCKE IN CONTEXT

The great question which, in all ages, has disturbed mankind, and brought on them the greatest part of their mischiefs . . . has been, not whether be power in the world, nor whence it came, but who should have it. —JOHN LOCKE (1632-1704)

The seventeenth century saw many important advances in legal theory on the continent. Hugo Grotius is best known today for his work on international law, but he also contributed to theories of natural rights along with Francisco Suárez and Samuel Freiherr von Pufendorf. Although continental legal and political theory only had a limited influence in the British Isles due to the differences between English and continental jurisprudence, Grotius's work on rights influenced several important thinkers in the Scottish Enlightenment. Among these was Francis Hutcheson, whose theories of unalienable rights shaped the thinking of many of the American Founders.

In the long run, however, the most important political theorist of the era in England was undoubtedly John Locke. To put Locke and his theories in context, we need to return to France during the Wars of Religion, continue through the era of Louis XIV, and then turn to the Stuart Restoration in England.

THE END OF THE WARS OF RELIGION IN FRANCE

When we last left France, we were in the middle of the Wars of Religion. Charles IX, the king at the time of the St. Bartholomew's Day massacres, died in 1574 without heir. He was succeeded by his brother, Henri III. Although Henri III supported the *Politiques* (Catholics who promoted a political solution to religious differences rather than war), the Wars of Religion continued, with the Catholic League, a new ultra-Catholic faction led by Henri de Lorraine, Duke of Guise, taking an increasingly prominent role in the wars. When Henri III's last surviving brother, François, Duke of Alençon, died, leaving Henri de Bourbon, King of Navarre and leader of the Huguenots, as Henri III's heir, public sentiment in France turned away from Henri III to Henri de Guise as the legitimate leader of France.

Like his brother Charles, Henri III was a weak person, and like many weak men he lashed out when he felt threatened. He invited Henri de Guise to a conference at his chateau at Amboise, and there he had his guards assassinate Henri and his brother Louis II, Cardinal of Guise, and imprison Henri's son. The Catholic League then turned against Henri III, the Parlement of Paris charged him with murder, and Henri III was forced to flee to his cousin Henri de Bourbon. The king and the Huguenots thus united against the Catholic League, which invited Spain to intervene in France to bring down Henri III.[1]

Henri III was assassinated by Jacques Clément, a Dominican friar, who was then killed by the king's guards. By normal laws of succession, this made the Protestant Henri de Bourbon the new king of France.

Henri de Bourbon proceeded to defeat the Catholic armies around France and took control of virtually the entire kingdom except Paris, which would never accept a Protestant king. Henri knew that without Paris, he would never be able to control France, and so he reputedly said, "Paris is worth a Mass," and converted to Catholicism.[2] The Catholic League cried foul, saying it was a trick and that the conversion was not real, but neither Paris nor the pope agreed. Paris opened its gates to Henri, and he was crowned Henri IV, the beginning of the Bourbon dynasty.

After uniting the Catholic and Protestant armies to drive out the Spanish, Henri IV's first major act was to issue the Edict of Nantes (1598). The Edict was intended to regulate the terms of debate between Catholics and Protestants in France: in essence, it said they would settle their differences with words, not cannons. The edict granted to Protestants the

1. The war occurring at this time was known as the War of the Three Henrys for reasons which should be obvious.

2. He never actually said that, but he did convert.

right to worship in certain places under certain conditions
and guaranteed their safety by providing them with a number
of fortified cities that they could hold in case the king tried
to renege on the guarantees given to them. The edict was to
remain in force in perpetuity until religious agreement was
reached within the kingdom.[3]

Henri IV was assassinated by a deranged ex-monk named
François Ravaillac, who was put to a gruesome end in an
unusually brutal public execution. Henri was succeeded by
his young son Louis XIII, though the government was run
primarily by his first minister, Armand du Plessis, Duke of
Richelieu, a cardinal in the Catholic Church and thus better
known simply as Cardinal Richelieu.

THE EROSION AND REVOCATION OF THE EDICT OF NANTES

Richelieu is important as a political theorist. The central
principle of his political philosophy was *raison d'état*, usually
translated literally but unhelpfully as "reason of state." *Raison
d'état* is the belief that the needs of the king overrule the needs
or rights of anyone else in the kingdom. This is the antithe-
sis in many ways of medieval feudalism, which decentralized
power and allowed a wide range of local privileges that over-
rode royal law. Richelieu thus put in place intendants, whose
job was to ride herd over the provincial governors who were
used to running their provinces as autonomous territories.

---

3. Although often presented as an early example of religious toleration, this was
not the goal of either side. Both wanted a religiously unified kingdom; they just
disagreed on what that religion should be.

In other words, he put restrictions on the nobility. Even as a cardinal in the Catholic Church, he supported the Protestant side against the Catholic Holy Roman emperor in the Thirty Years' War, since increasing the power of the Habsburgs would be bad for France.

He also went after the Huguenots, who claimed that not even the king could take away their rights, because the terms of the Edict of Nantes were in place "in perpetuity." Richelieu thus engineered a provocation that led the Huguenots to muster their armies in their fortified cities. Richelieu then besieged those cities and took them one by one, leaving the Huguenots with no defenses. And then . . . he stopped. His goal was not to eliminate the Huguenots but to put them in direct dependence on the goodwill of the king. That was all *raison d'état* demanded.

Louis XIII's successor, Louis XIV, was not so generous.

Louis XIV was the most successful absolutist monarch in early modern Europe. He learned statecraft form Cardinal Jules Mazarin, a protégé of Richelieu. Unlike other kings, he ran the state as his own prime minister and did so very effectively. The details of Louis XIV's reign need not detain us here. The key points are, first, that the sons of Charles I of England went into exile at Louis's court, where they were welcomed and shielded; they thus had Louis as a model of effective kingship. Second, Louis decided that the existence of a religious minority within his kingdom called into question his absolute rule.

Louis decided that the best way to solve this problem was to focus on the *until* clause of the Edict of Nantes: The edict would be in effect *until* religious agreement was reached. He began a program of increasing persecution of the Protestants in the kingdom, most famously through the use of *dragonnades*. In a *dragonnade*, a company of dragoons (i.e., mounted infantrymen) would move into a village and would be billeted in Protestant homes. The dragoons were instructed to do as much damage to the house and family as possible. Stores were ruined, property stolen, furniture, household goods, even buildings were damaged or destroyed, members of the family attacked. In short order, the family would be bankrupted or worse, and then the dragoon would move on to the next Protestant household. To keep from being forced to billet the soldiers, all you needed to do was convert to Catholicism.

Many did—so many, in fact, that Louis declared the terms of the Edict of Nantes fulfilled: there were no Protestants left in the kingdom (or so he claimed; there were up to a million left in what the Huguenots call "the church of the desert"). And so, in 1685, Louis revoked the Edict of Nantes.

Louis also banned Huguenot emigration except for pastors, but many escaped to other Protestant countries, bringing with them skills, capital, and stories about Louis's brutality. These stories of Louis's actions leading up to and including the revocation would have profound effect on politics across the channel in England.

THE STUART RESTORATION AND THE GLORIOUS REVOLUTION

In England, a Puritan Commonwealth had been put in place after the execution of Charles I in the English Civil

War. The Commonwealth came to an end in 1660 with the Stuart Restoration. Charles II, the son of Charles I, was brought back from France and made king. Beginning with the Act of Uniformity (1661), strict Anglicanism was enforced in England. Many Puritan leaders were jailed, and dissenters from the Church of England were persecuted. Even the Church of Scotland was suppressed, resulting in periodic armed rebellions.

In 1662, Charles II married Catherine of Braganza, the daughter of John IV of Portugal and a staunch Catholic. Her Catholicism made her unpopular in England. Aside from the religious issues, Catholicism was associated with tyranny: Elizabeth I's great enemy Philip II of Spain was Catholic, and Elizabethan propaganda portrayed him as a ruthless tyrant.[4] Also, Louis XIV was an absolute monarch, which looked like tyranny to people used to parliamentary rule—and this was even before the *dragonnades* began in 1681. And of course, everyone knew the pope was the antichrist, a tyrant.

When Charles II died in 1685, he was succeeded by his brother, James II. James was well received throughout the kingdom even though he had converted to Catholicism in the late 1660s. The population was willing to overlook his personal religious beliefs as long as he did not impose Catholicism on the kingdom. But then he began to appoint Catholics illegally into high positions in the government, justifying this through an edict declaring liberty of conscience to Catholics and Protestant dissenters (1687). When Anglican

4. This is the origin of the "Black Legend," which continues to this day to portray people from Spanish cultures negatively.

bishops protested, he had them arrested and charged with seditious libel—and this just two years after Louis XIV revoked the Edict of Nantes, criminalizing Protestantism.

And then James committed the unforgivable sin: he had a son who would be his heir, pushing his Protestant daughter Mary and her husband, William III of Orange, a Dutch prince, out of the line of succession. By this point, the English were well informed about Huguenot persecution in France and the revocation of the Edict of Nantes, all of which reinforced the idea that Catholicism was intrinsically tyrannical.[5] As a result, the English were not about to accept a Catholic dynasty, so a group of Protestant nobles invited William and Mary to take the throne (1688). William assembled an army and invaded England, and many Protestant officers in the English army defected to William's side. James lost his nerve and fled, throwing the royal seal into the Thames. He was captured, but to keep him from becoming a martyr and to avoid a repeat of the regicide of the English Civil War, William let him escape. James returned to France, where he was welcomed by Louis XIV and given refuge and a pension.

The accession to the throne of William and Mary is known as the Glorious Revolution since it was accomplished with almost no bloodshed. The following year (1689), William and Mary worked with Parliament to legitimize their

---

5. Very few scholars recognize the connection between the Revocation of the Edict of Nantes and the Glorious Revolution, but given the timing, the widespread reports of Catholic atrocities against the Huguenots, and the Huguenot diaspora in England, at the very least we can say that Louis XIV's actions contributed to the anti-Catholic attitude behind the Glorious Revolution.

government. Parliament decided that throwing the royal seal into the Thames was a de facto abdication, so they could offer the throne to Mary as queen with William, her husband, as king. Parliament also issued the Bill of Rights, which set up a constitutional monarchy and guaranteed parliamentary rights. William and Mary followed up by issuing the Edict of Toleration (also 1689), which declared religious freedom for all Trinitarian Protestants (but not Unitarians or Catholics).

JOHN LOCKE: PSYCHOLOGY AND POLITICS

The principle theorist of the Glorious Revolution was John Locke. Locke started out as a Puritan, but after reading a debate on the authorship of the Pentateuch (an early example of biblical criticism), Locke began to question not simply his Puritan background but the authority of Scripture. This led him to reject some ideas of traditional orthodox theology.

We see this in Locke's ideas on psychology, which were highly influential in the late seventeenth and eighteenth centuries and continue to influence some schools of psychology today. Locke argued that we are born as a *tabula rasa*, a blank slate. We have no innate ideas, no preprogrammed tendencies or inclinations.[6] As we go through life, our minds organize and categorize our experiences, and this is what shapes our thinking and our understanding of the world.

---

6. We know now that this is not true. For example, babies are preprogrammed to recognize human faces.

Locke's psychological ideas have obvious implications for education: children should be exposed to as wide a range of experiences as possible as early as possible because this will enhance their intelligence. But its implications extend well beyond this. Academic subjects had historically been understood as arranged in a hierarchy, with some as more basic and foundational than others but all related to each other in a hierarchy under theology, the queen of the sciences. But if Locke is right, this entire approach to structuring knowledge is nothing more than an arbitrary convention. Thus, in the eighteenth century, Denis Diderot and Jean le Rond d'Alembert edited a massive encyclopedia, a complete compendium of human knowledge with a distinctly Enlightenment spin. Unlike previous encyclopedias, however, this one was not arranged topically but alphabetically, an intentional statement that it was up to the reader to make connections between subjects rather than following an arbitrary, artificial system developed by someone else.

Locke's psychology also had implications for theology and, therefore, indirectly for politics. This is where his religious heterodoxy enters the picture. Locke's rejection of innate ideas meant that he rejected the doctrine of original sin, since that would imply an innate structure within us that inclined us toward sin. But if original sin is no longer an issue, then, in principle, humanity is perfectible: we can eliminate most corruption and "sin" by controlling the environment and the experiences that people have in order to minimize their opportunity to internalize corrupt behavior. And this in turn has implications for government. For example, Locke wrote a constitution for the Carolina colonies in 1669 that was about twice the length of the U.S. Constitution written a century later. The Carolina Constitution was so long because Locke believed that if he put in place an elaborate political structure that regulated every situation he could envision arising, it would create an environment in which corruption would be far less likely. The environment and the procedures would be conducive to virtue, and thus the governing officials would be pushed almost unconsciously into virtuous behavior. This would contrast sharply with the approach taken by the U.S. Constitution in 1787.

THE *TWO TREATISES OF GOVERNMENT*

Locke's most important contribution to political theory was not his psychology, but the remarkable synthesis of previous ideas about government and politics in his *Two Treatises of Government* (1689). What is rarely appreciated about Locke's work here is the way it synthesizes so many earlier ideas—unalienable rights (including specifically those already identified by medieval theologians), Protestant resistance theory, and a secularized version of the covenantal theory of government in the form of social contract theory—into a coherent whole that spelled the death of absolutism in England.

In his lesser known First Treatise, Locke takes on Sir Robert Filmer's book *Patriarcha*, a defense of absolutism and hereditary monarchy based on the biblical Adam's ownership of the world and his absolute authority over his children, which Adam then passed down to his heirs. Locke musters a variety of arguments against this: First, assuming fathers have authority, it is found in the begetting of children and cannot be passed on, since only God can create life. Second, Adam's authority over his children was not absolute but was shared with Eve. Third, following earlier thinkers, Locke denied that Adam owned the earth, saying that in the state of nature people owned all things in common. Fourth, even if you grant ownership, Adam's authority extended only to the animals, not people, and thus slavery and, with it, absolute authority over another human being is against the law of nature. Finally, and most tellingly in a culture that maintained primogeniture, Locke argued that Adam's rule could only be passed down to one person, who could only pass it to one person, and so on through all the generations. If Filmer was right, there would be only one universal king over the entire earth. But how would you figure out who that was?

The First Treatise is thus a rejection of absolutism, particularly in its patriarchal form. Locke's Second Treatise elaborates on his ideas about the proper principles for the establishment of government. For Locke, it begins with the state of nature.

Unlike Hobbes, who saw the state of nature only as a theoretical possibility, Locke argued that the original state of humanity was in fact a state of nature in which there was no government and no one had coercive power over another. All people were equal and were free. For Hobbes, such a state would lead immediately to a war of all against all, but Locke disagreed. Locke believed that even without government, people were still subject to divine and natural law and that people had the right to judge and punish breaches of those laws. In other words, people had liberty in the old sense—freedom to act as they wished within the boundaries set by God's law and natural law. No one had the right to tell anyone what to do within those boundaries, but neither did anyone have freedom to transgress those boundaries and violate the law.[7]

In his description of the state of nature, Locke echoed aspects of the medieval canonists' and theologians' discussions of humanity before the Fall: we were in a state of liberty where everything necessary for human flourishing was freely available. In his First Treatise, Locke had discussed Adam's pre-Fall state, emphasizing that he was not sovereign over the earth and that he did not have absolute authority over his children; they had liberty just as he did. This argument was aimed against absolutism, particularly as rooted in patriarchy. In the Second Treatise, he makes similar points regarding slavery and right of conquest, both of which were related to absolutism: absolutists justified absolute rule by right of conquest, and opponents of absolutism argued that it effectively reduced subjects to slaves. Locke says that slavery as it exists in the real world is illegitimate, since our right to liberty

7. Locke says we know natural law through the use of reason, but since in his psychology we are born as blank slates and construct our understanding of the world based on our experiences, it is not clear how reason can give us knowledge of natural law: in principle, everyone's reason could be different based on different experiences. Locke is benefiting here from a culture with strong Christian roots that influences even people who reject the fundamentals of the faith.

is unalienable (we cannot renounce it ourselves nor can it be taken from us).[8] Similarly, right of conquest only gives legitimate authority over combatants, not their families or possessions, and can only justly take reparations for the actual costs of the war.

Unlike Locke's medieval predecessors, however, he did not argue that everything was held in common in the state of nature: property, meaning things that are properly your own, existed from the beginning. For Locke, property included life, liberty, and estate, the last of which is property in the modern sense of the word. The idea of a right to life goes back to the Stoics. Locke followed Christian theologians on this point by arguing that, properly speaking, our life is not our own but belongs to God, and thus our right to life is unalienable. For the same reason, liberty, which was granted by God, is also unalienable—we cannot voluntarily renounce it and become a slave, and, by implication, we are obligated to defend our liberty against threats to it.

Locke's argument for a right to property deserves a closer look. As we saw earlier, the right to property was first articulated by Franciscan theologians, ironically to defend their right to renounce property. Their argumentation was based on canon law. Locke was strongly anti-Catholic, so he could not rely on the canonists for an argument for property rights. Instead, he began his argument with what

8. The only legitimate form of slavery according to Locke is a consequence of committing a crime worthy of the death sentence. In this circumstance, the offended party or group can commute the sentence to slavery since slavery is no worse a punishment than death.

is properly our own, in other words, with ourselves. He argued that when we work to produce something, we put part of ourselves into it through our labor. As a result, it is now in a sense part of ourselves, and for this reason, we have a right to own what we produce as long as by taking ownership we do not deprive others of their right to obtain property themselves.[9] This idea is known as the labor theory of property.[10]

According to Locke, in the state of nature, we have the right to protect our property in accordance with the laws of nature and of God and to punish those who violate that right or any other aspect of natural or divine law. And this right to punish is ultimately the origin of human governments. A majority of the people in a region decide to establish a government to protect their rights and property, both of which are prepolitical (i.e., originating before the establishment of human government) and thus not subject to governmental authority. The people contract[11] with the government—whether a monarchy, an aristocracy, or a republic—and agree to obey its laws if it protects their property.

Should the government violate the rights of its citizens, the people have the right and sometimes the obligation to revolt. Locke is worth quoting in detail here:

9. Adam Smith's *The Wealth of Nations* (1776) puts a similar restriction on ownership in its vision of a free-market system.

10. Although Locke does not use this argument, the same principle is at work in Genesis 2: Adam is told to tend the Garden of Eden and to eat the fruit it produces; he thus is literally entitled to the fruit of his labor.

11. Notice I did not use the word *covenant*. Like Hobbes, Locke secularized the Calvinist idea of covenantal government.

The reason why men enter into society, is the preservation of their property; and the end why they choose and authorize a legislative, is, that there may be laws made, and rules set, as guards and fences to the properties of all the members of the society: to limit the power, and moderate the dominion, of every part and member of the society: for since it can never be supposed to be the will of the society, that the legislative should have a power to destroy that which every one designs to secure by entering into society, and for which the people submitted themselves to legislators of their own making; whenever the legislators endeavour to take away and destroy the property of the people, or to reduce them to slavery under arbitrary power, they put into a state of war with the people, who are thereupon absolved from any farther obedience, and are left to the common refuge, which God hath provided for all men, against force and violence. Whensoever therefore the legislative shall transgress this fundamental rule of society; and either by ambition, fear, folly or corruption, endeavour to grasp themselves, or put into the hands of any other, an absolute power over the lives, liberties, and estates of the people; by this breach of trust they forfeit the power the people had put into their hands for quite contrary ends, and it devolves to the people, who have a right to resume their original liberty, and, by the establishment of a new legislative, (such as they shall think fit) provide for their own safety and security, which is the end for which they are in society. What I have said here, concerning the legislative in general, holds true also concerning the supreme executor, who having a double trust put in him, both to have a part in the legislative, and the supreme execution of the law, acts against both, when he goes about to set up his own arbitrary will as the law of the society. He acts also contrary to his trust, when he either employs the force, treasure, and offices of the society to corrupt the representatives, and gain them to his purposes; or openly pre-engages the electors, and prescribes to their choice, such, whom he has, by solicitations, threats, promises, or otherwise, won to his designs: and employs them to bring in such, who have promised beforehand what to vote, and what to enact.[12]

Locke thus argues that when the government oversteps its limits and infringes on the property of the people, they have the right to rebel, to dissolve the contract binding them to the government, and to establish a new government that will protect their rights. Once again, this is in direct contradiction to Hobbes and other absolutist theorists who argue that there is never a right to revolt and that the government, by definition, cannot do anything illegal or trample on the rights of citizens (thereby implying that rights are granted by the government and not by God). Locke also follows a peculiarly British take on resistance theory that enshrines the right of resistance on the people and not in the lesser magistrate.

12. John Locke, *Two Treatises of Government* (London: C. and J. Rivington et al., 1824), 261–262.

IMPLICATIONS

Locke's great accomplishment in the *Two Treatises of Government* is the unification of multiple elements of legal and political theory into a single coherent philosophy of government. He develops an original, reason-based justification for the natural rights identified by medieval theologians and canonists and integrates it into a secularized version of Reformed ideas of covenantal government. This involves a quasi-Augustinian emphasis on limited government divorced from its roots in Augustine's doctrine of original sin. From this base, he further develops ideas with their roots in Protestant resistance theory to explain when and why it is legitimate to resist and replace governments that have turned tyrannical, which, according to Locke, occurs when they have violated the unalienable rights of the citizens or the laws of nature and nature's God. He puts it succinctly: "Revolt is the right of the people." The roots of his thought are thus firmly within the Christian tradition, though in many ways Locke followed Hobbes's lead by secularizing the earlier ideas. Nonetheless, Locke continued to recognize God as the Creator and as the source of human rights.

The *Two Treatises* were also very topical. They refuted absolutist arguments based on patriarchy and divine right, in effect slaying Leviathan without explicitly mentioning Hobbes, and provided a theoretical justification for the Glorious Revolution that had taken place just three years before they were published. Given the English assumption that Catholicism equals tyranny, in overthrowing James II the English were simply defending their unalienable right

to liberty. Further, in promulgating the Edict of Toleration, William and Mary were simultaneously defending
the liberty of the people of England by officially tolerating
all Trinitarian Protestants while protecting them from the
threat of Catholic tyranny.

The irony is that although the *Two Treatises* were written specifically to address the situation in England, their
most important impact was across the Atlantic Ocean in the
American colonies, where they shaped the political thought
and argumentation of Thomas Jefferson and the Declaration
of Independence.

CHAPTER 9
THE AMERICAN FOUNDERS

The aim of every political Constitution, is or ought to be first to obtain for rulers men who possess most wisdom to discern, and most virtue to pursue, the common good of society; and in the next place, to take the most effectual precautions for keeping them virtuous whilst they continue to hold their public trust.

—JAMES MADISON (1751-1836)

As we have seen, John Locke's *Two Treatises of Government* combined many elements of Christian political theology into a coherent but largely secularized whole. Few if any of Locke's core ideas were completely original; his genius came from how he combined Augustinian ideas on the necessity of limited government (divorced from their theological context in the doctrine of original sin), natural rights theory (based on reason rather than canon law), covenantal theories of government (secularized as social contract theory), liberty of conscience (except for Catholics), and Protestant resistance theory into a unified theory of government. Remarkably, however, his ideas had little influence in England itself, perhaps because the Glorious Revolution was already a fait accompli. Their greatest impact came in England's colonies in America, specifically in influencing Thomas Jefferson and the American Declaration of Independence.

Before we get to Jefferson, however, the New England colonies deserve a closer look. New England was the cradle of the Revolution, and its political ideas were influenced far more by the Puritan political tradition and by the Great Awakening than by Locke.

THE GREAT AWAKENING AND POLITICS

Although we think of the Great Awakening primarily in terms of Jonathan Edwards and "Sinners in the Hands of an Angry God," it was part of a much wider movement in the British world that had implications that went well beyond questions of personal salvation. In Britain, the faith had been reduced to a number of pro forma activities: attend church on Sunday, get married in the church, have your children baptized, have a church funeral, be buried in the churchyard, and not much else. As an Anglican friend once told me, "The beauty of being an Anglican is you don't actually have to *do* anything." In fact, taking your faith more seriously was seen as "enthusiasm," a nasty word that was roughly equivalent to calling someone a Holy Roller or a fanatic today. Remember, England had just recently had a civil war over religious practice, and no one wanted a repeat performance.

In New England, Puritanism held on longer, but it too was becoming increasingly formalized. Originally, Puritans needed to be able to give a testimony of conversion to be a church member and to have their children baptized, but more and more, their children did not have such a testimony; they simply grew up with the norms of the church and never experienced conversion. To deal with this situation, the Puritans adopted the Half-Way Covenant (c. 1662), which allowed baptized children of church members to be considered full members of the church, thus allowing their children to be baptized. Historians differ on the significance of the Half-Way Covenant. Some see it as a move away from earlier Puritan sectarianism; others see it as marking the end of the Puritan vision of the church as a spotless body of converted believers. Whatever the correct interpretation of the Half-Way Covenant, the shift to hereditary church membership had the effect of watering down the Puritan theology of conversion. In the context of the eighteenth century, this led New England churches into an increasingly rationalistic approach to theology, more liberal congregational churches, and ultimately the rise of Unitarianism.

The increasingly rationalistic religion of New England and the purely formal religion of Britain were both challenged by a movement known as the Evangelical Revival. In Britain, this took the form of the Welsh Revivals under Howell Harris and the Methodist Revivals in both their Calvinistic form (e.g., George Whitefield) and their Arminian form (e.g., the Wesleys). The Great Awakening was the expression of the Evangelical Revival in the colonies.

Evangelicalism in this period had significant political overtones. In England, the crucial point was an emphasis on social action, on rooting out sin not just in the individual's life but in society. This would be a critical element in British abolitionism and in the wide range of social reform movements that emerged in the late eighteenth and early nineteenth centuries. Many scholars believe that these developments were critical in preventing England from following France into a violent revolution aimed at overturning church, state, and the entire social order. Discussing that in any detail would take us too far afield for present purposes.

In the American colonies, the emphasis on conversion would have the biggest impact politically in the long run. In New England, Congregational churches divided between New Light churches that supported the revival and Old Light churches that opposed it. For supporters of revival, your position and your credentials did not matter, only that you had yourself been converted. Thus, a member of the congregation who had a conversion experience had more spiritual authority than a minister or, in Anglican areas, a bishop who had not been converted. In fact, George Whitefield and Gilbert Tennent both warned about the dangers of an unconverted ministry. Pastors who had not received the new birth were still dead in trespasses and sins, and it was hazardous to listen to and take spiritual counsel from dead men.

This had enormous practical implications extending well beyond the church. First, it promoted egalitarianism and individualism, both of which undermined aspects of covenantal ideas about society. The common view at the time was that God had established a covenant with the people and their rulers that they would obey His laws. From there, the rulers made a covenant with the people to enforce and obey natural and divine law, to make laws in accordance with them, to defend the people, etc., and the people in turn agreed to obey their rulers.[1] This second covenant included the political hierarchy, not just the king. Thus, in traditional Protestant resistance theory, the lesser magistrates who were part of this second covenant were authorized to lead resistance against the higher magistrates when there was need.

Yet in the revivals, people saw God as working directly with individuals, not through covenants or social and political hierarchies. This meant that the individual—especially the converted individual—had as much authority in God's eyes as kings or bishops. This reinforced the tendencies already present in British versions of resistance theory to vest the right of resistance in the private citizen, not the lesser magistrate.

1. This idea was first clearly articulated in *Vindiciae contra tyrannos* (1579), discussed last chapter. Remember that *Vindiciae* was a Huguenot political treatise written in the wake of the St. Bartholomew's Day Massacres and translated into English in 1689, the year after the Glorious Revolution. Like Locke's *Two Treatises of Government*, which it influenced, it was published in England as a justification for the Glorious Revolution. The work was very popular across the ocean in New England.

This thinking worked against the fundamentally hierarchical understanding of the church, the political order, and society that was common in the day. If God can reach down to a servant or a slave but leave the pastor untouched, then the existing hierarchies in society were meaningless before God. And if they were meaningless before God, why should they hold sway in society or politics?

The Great Awakening also fostered a passion for liberty. Those converted during the revivals knew they had to live according to God's laws, but they also believed that, as people who had been born again and who had the Spirit, they could understand and interpret what the laws meant as well as any university-trained pastor or theologian. Another characteristic of Evangelicalism was biblicism, and anything they did not see warrant for in Scripture they felt free to reject. This included not just religious ceremonies and practices with inadequate scriptural support in their eyes, but also constraints on their liberty imposed by kings and governors. Thus, the New England colonies established public schools for the express purpose of teaching literacy so that citizens could challenge their legislators for the scriptural justification of the laws that they passed. Laws without scriptural warrant needed to be repealed as violations of Christian liberty.

The idea of Christian liberty was rapidly transmuted into a passion for political liberty in the areas influenced by the Great Awakening. We will take a closer look at what liberty meant in its eighteenth-century context, but first we will turn to Jefferson's thinking embodied in the Declaration of Independence.

THE DECLARATION OF INDEPENDENCE

Once the Revolutionary War broke out in New England, the Continental Congress meeting in Philadelphia assigned Jefferson to write a defense of the actions of the colonists and why they had a right to declare themselves free and independent of Britain. Rather than using the kind of Calvinist resistance theory we see in New England, Jefferson turned to Locke for his justification of the Revolution.

The preamble to the Declaration of Independence includes a succinct summary of Locke's theories of government:

> We hold these truths to be self-evident, that all men are created equal, that they are endowed, by their Creator, with certain unalienable Rights, that among these are Life, Liberty, and the pursuit of Happiness,[2] That to secure these rights, Governments are instituted among Men, deriving their just powers from the consent of the governed, That whenever any Form of Government becomes destructive of these ends, it is the Right of the People to alter or abolish it, and to institute new Government, laying its foundation on such principles, and organizing its powers in such form, as to them shall seem most likely to effect their Safety and Happiness.

2. This clause is usually punctuated incorrectly. In the original, there is a comma at this point; however, an early printing put a period here, and that has become the most common version of the preamble. The period, however, distorts the intent: Jefferson is arguing that this entire summary of Locke's views on government is a self-evident truth.

Jefferson here articulates the core elements of Locke's theories discussed in the last chapter. A few things are worth noting.

Jefferson echoes Locke's insistence that the origin of human rights is found in God rather than government. For all his secularizing tendencies, Locke never forgot that our rights are unalienable (so the government has no authority over them) because they come from God himself. Jefferson, even less of an orthodox Christian than Locke,[3] also affirmed this as necessary for the protection of our rights from government encroachment.

Locke identified our unalienable rights as life, liberty, and estate; Jefferson modified this list to life, liberty, and the pursuit of happiness. The right to life is uncontroversial and can be traced back to classical philosophy. Given the importance of liberty to the Founders, it deserves a closer look.

The classical definition of liberty is the freedom to act as one wills within the bounds set by natural and divine law and the laws of the state. In the Christian tradition, the laws of the state were supposed to conform to natural law, or they were unjust. For Hobbes and other absolutist theorists, however, the will of the king has the force of law; the king thus cannot act illegally nor trample on a subject's rights or liberty. Absolutism effectively makes liberty a dead letter.

To defend the right to liberty against the encroachments of absolutism, there was a renewed insistence on natural and

---

3. Jefferson is often described as a Deist. This is not accurate. He was a Unitarian rationalist: he believed that God could and did intervene in the affairs of men, something no true Deist could affirm.

divine law as a boundary the sovereign could not transgress. Further, there was a growing emphasis on what philosophers now refer to as positive freedom, that is, freedom *to* or freedom *for* rather than freedom *from*. Specifically, liberty referred to the freedom to pursue good ends of your own choice within the bounds of natural and divine law. Liberty thus included a moral imperative: the only legitimate ends had to be virtuous themselves and had to be pursued by virtuous means.

Virtue was an important word to the Founders. For centuries, it had been recognized that virtue was essential to the survival of a republic, because without virtue people begin to make decisions out of greed, pride, self-interest . . . and the result is inevitably the collapse of the republic. True liberty must therefore be undergirded by a virtuous population, and liberty must be used to develop and promote virtue.[4]

The alternative to liberty is license. License is negative freedom, that is, freedom from restraint. Licentious people pursue their desires without regard for any rules or restrictions on their behavior. Freedom to them means that no one can tell them what to do or to tell them that what they are doing is wrong.

No political thinker in the centuries leading up to the Founders believed that we had a natural right to license, only to liberty. And yet today, freedom is overwhelmingly understood as negative freedom, as license. What happened?

---

4. The root word of virtue is the Latin *vir*, meaning a responsible adult male—a husband, soldier, etc. In the Roman world, slaves were not *viri*—they were not responsible and thus lacked virtue, which could only be developed in the context of freedom.

The complete answer is long and complicated, but the short version is that the rise of moral and cultural relativism killed liberty. If relativism is true, there is no natural or divine law and no boundaries within which to operate. There is no proper purpose to use our freedom for—only our personal choices operating within a moral vacuum. Virtue, in the classical sense of character traits that are intrinsically good, was understood by the Founders as necessary for a republic, yet in a world where there are no intrinsic goods, virtue is dead. And if there is no virtue, there can be no liberty. Freedom has no purpose and is reduced to solipsistic license.

The connection of liberty to virtue brings us to Jefferson's third unalienable right, the right to pursue happiness, replacing Locke's right to property. Our current usage of the word *happiness* is far from Jefferson's intended meaning. *Happiness* was Jefferson's translation of the ancient Greek word *eudaimonia*, which you might remember from chapter 3 as an important element of Greek ethics and, according to Aristotle, the purpose of life itself. *Eudaimonia* is a life well-lived, a good life in every sense of the word. Achieving *eudaimonia* required the use of reason and the cultivation of *areté*, "virtue" or "excellence." And since *eudaimonia* is the purpose of life, our right to pursue it must be unalienable, prepolitical and thus not subject to state authority.

Jefferson argued that we have an unalienable right to pursue a life of excellence in all things, including moral excellence and virtue. This is closely connected to our right to liberty, since *eudaimonia*, the purpose of life, implies virtue which can only be obtained if we have liberty. Jefferson's

understanding of the pursuit of happiness also sneaks property rights in through the back door: to live a life of excellence requires productive property, which gives us the
means and opportunity to pursue *eudaimonia*. Further, Jefferson believed that the best school of *areté* was to work
your own land. He believed that the yeoman farmer was
the best type of citizen in a republic, since farming required
discipline, diligence, prudence, hard work, patience . . . all
the virtues. He did not think much of the cities and doubt-
ed that the "swinish masses" in them would ever be able to
govern themselves.

After the preamble, the body of the Declaration lists ways
that George III violated the unalienable rights of the American colonies. Then it concludes that they are justified in dis-
solving their connection with him and setting up their own
government. The specific details need not detain us here.

THE CONSTITUTION

To round out this chapter (and this book), we should look
at some of the often-overlooked aspects of the government
that the newly formed United States of America would ultimately adopt.

After winning their independence, the various colo-
nies-turned-states set up the first national government with
the Articles of Confederation. This was designed to maintain the autonomy of the individual states. In fact, it did this
so well that it had an unworkably weak government at the
federal level with absolutely minimal responsibilities and

powers. As a result, the Federalists began to meet to work out a new system of government that would still maintain much of the autonomy of the states in their internal affairs but with a stronger federal government to deal with issues that went beyond the legitimate purview of any single state.

The basic concept for this was pioneered by the French Reformed churches, which initially developed the Presbyterian system of church government to handle a similar situation in attempting to unite a group of churches that jealously guarded their independence. The resulting system was remarkably effective and was adopted by both the Dutch Reformed and the (Presbyterian) Church of Scotland. From Presbyterianism, it influenced several important figures among the American Founders.

The result, of course, was the Constitution of the United States.

The Federalists were remarkably well educated and knew their political theory, history, and theology. They also knew that because they were establishing a new government in a context where there had been none before, they were free to design it any way they wanted to. Unlike the Glorious Revolution, which was a conservative revolution trying to preserve English tradition, or the French Revolution, which was a radical revolution intending to sweep away everything about the past, the American Revolution can be seen as a moderate revolution, free to keep what it wanted from the past but also free to get rid of what it did not like. This type of revolution is likely only possible in a newly emerging country without a long political tradition to defend or attack.

Not surprisingly, Aristotle was an important influence on the structure of the government they devised. As we have seen, Artistotle's three basic types of government existed in both positive and degenerate forms: monarchy/tyranny; aristocracy/oligarchy; republic/democracy. Each has its strengths and weaknesses, so the ideal state is a mixed state that combines elements of all three. Following these principles, the framers designed the Constitution to incorporate all three types of government recognized by Aristotle: the monarchial principle is embodied in the presidency, the aristocratic principle in the Senate as a deliberative body representing the states, and the republican principle in the House of Representatives, where the people themselves have direct representation.

Along with the strengths of one branch making up for the weaknesses in others, this system in theory provided a system of checks and balances in the government. The Federalists were influenced not just by Aristotle but by Augustine: they knew that original sin infects everyone, so no individual and no institution can be trusted with absolute power. That is, no one can operate without oversight. And so, among these three governmental institutions, if one should attempt to overstep its proper authority, the other two could step in and stop it, with the judiciary acting as referee. Interestingly, not only was this system inspired by the problem of original sin operating in government, but it actually used original sin to its advantage: it assumed that members of each institution would be so interested in preserving their own powers and prerogatives that they would naturally band together to stop encroachments by the other branches of government. In other words, lust for power in each institution would cause it to block any other institution from expanding its power beyond its constitutional boundaries.

This brings us to a second element of the original Constitution that we often overlook today: its rejection of political parties. From at least the rise of the city republics in medieval Italy, factions were recognized as inherently dangerous. By the early modern period, they were recognized as the death of republics. The framers of the Constitution understood this and feared the rise of factions within the government. Thus, in the original form of the Constitution, the president was the candidate who received the most electoral votes and the vice president the candidate who received the second highest electoral vote total. It is hard to imagine what the executive would look like if we had had this system in recent presidential elections. It was soon recognized that this system was unworkable, so it was changed to an election for a slate of candidates for president and vice president.

The attempt to block factions, also known as political parties, was a crucial element in the system of checks and balances between the various institutions in the government. As long as each institution retained the loyalty of its members so that they would act as a check against other branches, the system had a chance of working. If political parties emerged, however, the framers feared that loyalty to party would overrule loyalty to institution, and thus that coalitions across institutional lines would develop that would prevent the system from working correctly: people would turn a blind eye to abuses of their own party but would do everything to thwart even legitimate actions by another party for pure partisan advantage. That concern proved remarkably and unfortunately prescient.

Ultimately, however, the framers knew that they could not develop a system that was proof against corruption. Many were descendants of Puritans, after all, and even those who were not recognized the pervasiveness of human sin and the potential for twisting even the best-designed institutions to serve corrupt ends. That is why the Constitution of the United States is shorter than Locke's Constitution for the Carolinas: Locke thought he could design a system that could stop corruption; the framers realized that the best they could do is set up a system that would make corruption difficult. They argued that, in the end, the only defense the government would have against corruption would be to elect virtuous people to office. Once again, we see the importance of virtue to a republic. A republic only stands if it consists of virtuous people who do not seek from government what it should not give, and virtuous political leaders who subordinate their own interests to the good of the commonwealth.

THE BILL OF RIGHTS

When the Constitution was ratified, political thinkers in Europe were impressed. Already in 1787, a course on the Constitution of the United States was offered at the free Lycée de Paris by the lawyer Jacques-Vincent Delacroix. From their perspective, it looked like the rustics in America had created the perfect Aristotelian mixed state, something the Europeans had been trying to do for centuries. The Constitution would become an inspiration for new forms of government emerging in Europe throughout the nineteenth century.

But before that could happen, the Constitution needed to be ratified. Some states refused to ratify it unless it included a Bill of Rights—something the framers were hesitant to add because they were afraid it would be seen as an enumeration of the only rights guaranteed by the Constitution. (This is, in fact, how most people view the Bill of Rights today, considering anything not explicitly mentioned—or found in its "penumbra" by the Supreme Court—to be subject to the federal government.) Nonetheless, the Constitution could not be passed without it, so the first ten amendments of the Constitution were passed at the same time the Constitution was ratified.

This is not the place for a complete study of the Bill of Rights, although a few points are worth highlighting. The Bill of Rights deals with negative rights, things that the government cannot infringe upon. The point is that the rights are not granted by the government but are granted by God, and thus the government has no right to suppress them.

The Bill of Rights begins with a statement on religious freedom: "Congress shall pass no law respecting an establishment of religion, or prohibiting the free exercise thereof." From there, the amendment forbids Congress from abridging the right to free speech, freedom of the press, peaceable assembly, and petitioning the government to redress grievances. Several elements of this amendment are worth noting. First, an establishment of religion in this context refers to establishing a national church. Given the diversity of denominations in the United States, this prevented Congress from picking one for the entire nation. James Madison, the architect of this amendment, believed that religion would flourish best in a free marketplace of ideas, so this amendment was written to encourage religious flourishing, not to stifle it. It is also worth noting that the prohibition was originally limited to Congress. Several states had established churches and continued to have them for decades after the Constitution was ratified. The issue was a national church, not state churches.

The free exercise clause is foundational to the rest of this amendment and to several others. Free exercise refers to the right to live according to our deepest beliefs. Without that, freedom of speech and the press are meaningless: we could be prohibited from speaking or writing about the things that matter the most to us. We might be able to assemble, but only for approved purposes, not for religious reasons. And we would have no inherent right to protest any of these prohibitions—maybe other things, but not this.

At its heart, the free exercise clause is about freedom of conscience, an idea with deep Christian roots going back through Luther to the early church fathers. Unfortunately, it has been applied only inconsistently over the centuries by Christians. If we are to be taken seriously, we need to insist on religious freedom for all, not just ourselves.

As I write this, we have Democratic politicians who describe freedom of religion as nothing more than an excuse for bigotry; we also see polls that find support for freedom of religion in steep decline, particularly among younger people.

What they do not understand or refuse to acknowledge is that if you remove or revise the free exercise clause, you gut the entire first amendment and make the rest of the Bill of Rights meaningless.

A final point on the Bill of Rights involves the Tenth Amendment, which states that the powers of the federal government are few and are enumerated in the Constitution; all other powers are reserved for the people or the states. This amendment is a dead letter and has been for some time, arguably since the Civil War (and certainly throughout the twentieth century). Irrespective of the Tenth Amendment, the power of the federal government has been growing steadily. Its reach now touches virtually every area of life, its laws and regulations so voluminous that no one can know or understand all of them. As of 2019, there were 72,564 pages of federal regulations; if that seems like a lot, consider that it is down nearly 25,000 pages from its peak in 2016.[5] It has been estimated that the average American commits three felonies a day without even knowing it.[6]

IMPLICATIONS

The Constitution and the Bill of Rights were written to limit the power of government. They are intended to promote ordered liberty—liberty in the sense that we are to

---

5. Law Librarians of Washington, DC, "Federal Register Pages Published Annually," https://www.llsdc.org/assets/sourcebook/fed-reg-pages.pdf
6. Harvey Silverglate, *Three Felonies a Day: How the Feds Target the Innocent* (Encounter Books, 2011).

have freedom within the boundaries of the laws of God and nature, but ordered in the sense that government can set limits on our liberty in cases of great necessity. Liberty of conscience and its corollary, freedom of religion, deserve particular protection against governmental interference, since so many other freedoms depend on them.

And yet as I write this, we are witnessing government regulations interfering with even the most basic religious activities, including dictating when and where we can worship and even what we can and cannot do in our free exercise of our faith, while not holding secular groups or even the government itself to the same restrictions.

If the state can insinuate itself into religion, is there any area that can truly claim to be independent of state regulation? Government regulations dictate what can be taught in public schools, determine accreditation for non-government schools, determine what we can eat or drink, set rules for businesses that are not applied to all equally and thereby determine which businesses are likely to survive, set rules for hiring and firing, limit landlords' ability to collect rent, dictate what messages and even words are acceptable in media, set rules on acceptable forms of outdoor recreation in a pandemic . . . the list goes on and on and gets more and more specific. And in some areas, the government actively encourages people to report on their neighbors for violating the rules.

This is not the lifestyle of a free people. This is soft totalitarianism.

This is how Leviathan is reborn.

EPILOGUE

The cry "Liberty, equality, fraternity or death!" was much in vogue during the Revolution. Liberty ended by covering France with prisons, equality by multiplying titles and decorations, and fraternity by dividing us. Death alone prevailed. —LOUIS DE BONALD (1754–1840)

The founding documents of the United States—the Declaration of Independence and the Constitution—were the culmination and the highest expression of a long evolution of political thought among Christian thinkers going back to the early church. Many disparate elements of this tradition were brought together by John Locke, to which the framers of the Constitution reintroduced the Augustinian understanding of original sin and distrust of government that was so important to the system of checks and balances in the federal government. Although the U.S. government was designed without explicit reference to the Bible or Christianity, its core ideas have their roots in the Christian tradition.

It was also the last major accomplishment of that tradition.

Christianity was not the only influence on the Founders. Michael Novak argues that the American eagle flies on two wings: Christianity and the Enlightenment.[1] This is true of Locke as well. His ideas may have originated in Christian political theology, but he secularized them as much as possible, perhaps to avoid associating them with the Puritan revolutionaries of a previous generation, perhaps because of the fear of enthusiasm in the Anglican Church of his day, and certainly also because of the influence of early Enlightenment thought. He did cite the Bible when necessary to answer arguments of his opponents, so he was certainly not anti-Christian; nonetheless, his work was an important step toward the widespread acceptance of secular political thought.

The real turning point, however, came with the French Revolution. The French Enlightenment thinkers who inspired and led the Revolution wanted to reform society from top to bottom, and they saw the Catholic Church as a major obstacle that had to be eliminated to accomplish their goal. Voltaire, for example, had as his war cry, "*Écrassez l'infâme!*" ("Crush the infamous thing," meaning the Catholic Church). Then there were the words attributed to Jean Meslier: "I would like the last of the kings to be strangled with the guts of the last priest."

1. Michael Novak, *On Two Wings: Humble Faith and Common Sense at the American Founding* (San Francisco: Encounter Books, 2002).

To put it differently, they were not interested in anything coming from Christianity, only the secular rationalism of the Enlightenment.

The French revolutionaries believed that using reason, they could establish a new social order that was, for all intents and purposes, unconnected to the previous regime—a new system of government rejecting the absolutism of Louis XIV and his heirs and establishing a new social structure and a new economic system. The result was bloody chaos, with hundreds of thousands dead either by war or judicial murder. Of course, eventually a new, relatively stable system emerged with the help of another emperor, Napoleon. Even still, France was convulsed by periodic revolutions throughout the nineteenth century.

The French Revolution changed the nature of revolutions. Every revolution since has been purely secular, guided by reason and Enlightenment philosophy toward a secular utopia. And the result inevitably has been blood in the streets.

The reason is simple and rooted in a change in society explained by C.S. Lewis in *The Abolition of Man*: "For the wise men of old, the cardinal problem of human life was how to conform the soul to objective reality, and the solution was wisdom, self-discipline, and virtue. For the modern, the cardinal problem is how to conform reality to the wishes of man, and the solution is a technique."[2]

The desire to conform reality and thus society to the wishes of man is the heart of the French Revolution and all other

2. C.S. Lewis, *The Abolition of Man* (New York: Macmillan, 1943), 87–88.

attempts at creating a secular utopia. Traditional societies developed and evolved over millennia to try to find the best way to live in accordance with human nature, to conform ourselves and our society to reality rather than the other way around. There is wisdom in the old ways. Contrary to modernity, human nature is not infinitely malleable nor reducible to our philosophical ideas. Trying to change reality to fit our desires is a fool's errand, dooming its victims to lives of brokenness and disorder.

This attempt to force reality to align with our will has been an important part of modern American culture. Not surprisingly, it has also infected law and government. The Founders knew that the Constitution could only go so far in preventing corruption given humanity's fallen nature. The rise of political parties has disrupted the system of checks and balances as the Founders feared. However, the influence of modernity came primarily through the Supreme Court, the one institution in the federal government that was supposed to be independent of political pressures. The Court has adopted the idea of a "living Constitution" as well as the principle that laws need to be interpreted not according to their explicit intent, but in accordance with changing norms and standards in society. The result has been the Court's rewriting laws even though it is not supposed to have legislative power. Furthermore, as Thomas Jefferson predicted, the Court has turned the Constitution into "a nose of wax" that can be twisted and reshaped according to its desires. And in true dictatorial fashion, the Court's decrees cannot be challenged.

Another element in the movement toward modernity has been the rise of the regulatory state discussed in chapter 9. The vast majority of regulations—de facto laws—are written by unelected bureaucrats in the executive branch to interpret and apply laws passed by Congress. In effect, Congress has abdicated both its legislative responsibilities and its oversight of regulations, substituting the opinions of "experts" in the regulatory agencies for those of the representatives of the people. This rule by technocrats is what Lewis meant when he talked about technique being the solution to imposing our will on reality.

This rise of technocracy also marks the turn away from free markets toward socialism. Economic and political systems parallel each other: in free markets, we vote companies into business with our dollars, and we buy what politicians are selling when we vote for them; in socialism, the economy is directed by government experts and so is the rest of the political order. The rise of the regulatory state inevitably weakens free markets and representative government (since the representatives do not write the regulations).

As if the threat from the federal government were not enough, states and municipalities have added their own regulations into the mix. For example, in some places, it is illegal to collect the rainwater that falls on your house. These regulations even subvert rights expressly guaranteed in the Constitution: in New York City, Washington, D.C., and elsewhere, for example, during 2020's COVID-19 restrictions, churches were prohibited from meeting in direct violation of the First Amendment while Black Lives

Matter protests were permitted. In other words, freedom of peaceable assembly applied only to groups promoting approved messages.

The regulatory state, on all levels, is thus the biggest threat to liberty and republican government today. Its reach extends to all of life, limiting our freedom of action far more severely than natural or divine law does. The result is the rise of a soft totalitarianism that has given birth to a new Leviathan.

How are we to respond to the threats to liberty we are facing? Answering that question begins with this book. We are remarkably unaware of our own Christian history. What wisdom can we glean from thinking on rights, liberties, limited government, tyranny, and resistance from the Christian tradition?

First, we need to be clear on the difference between natural rights, generally known today as human rights, and civil rights. Natural rights are God-given and not subject to government control; civil rights are the specific rights we have as citizens of a country. Liberty is a natural right; voting is a civil right. The distinction is critical. Ironically, most people in America today seem to consider voting rights to be more fundamental than natural rights such as liberty of conscience. We must not make that mistake. Understanding the difference helps guide our response to attacks on our rights.

Second, resistance theory developed in the context of monarchies. In a republic, we have far more influence on government policy than most people could dream of in the sixteenth century. Our first step in response to attacks on our liberty is to use the legal means at our disposal to preserve our rights and the rights of others. We vote; we write letters to government officials; we educate; we seek to sway public opinion; if necessary, we sue. Working through the lesser magistrate is also a possibility: there have been instances of sheriffs refusing to enforce laws they believed to be unconstitutional.

Civil disobedience—disobeying the laws and accepting the consequences—is also an option, particularly if legal means are exhausted. Nonviolent resistance is a powerful tool in changing laws and social norms. This was true in the early church as well as during the Civil Rights Movement in the 1960s and elsewhere.

In light of the discussion of Protestant resistance theory and unalienable rights, the issue of active resistance inevitably arises. There is no question our unalienable rights are being eroded. Even leaving aside abortion, where is the right to life when people can be arrested for using force to defend their lives or the lives of loved ones? Where is the right to property when a city like Santa Monica is not even enforcing petty theft laws when less than nine hundred dollars is stolen? Where is the right to liberty in view of the increasing restrictions on our freedoms on the one hand while the state advocates license on the other?

These are genuine concerns, but because we are in a republic, we have options not available to those in early modern monarchies. Further, unlike the Schmalkaldic League, we are not facing the threat of war. Self-defense is justified today; active resistance to the government is not.

A last point: for Christians, we must never forget that
the most powerful tool at our disposal is corporate worship
and prayer. This was recognized by the Founders, including
Benjamin Franklin, probably the least religious of them all.
When faced with deadlock on numerous issues at the Constitutional Convention, he delivered this speech, which is
worth quoting in its entirety:

> Mr. President, the small progress we have made after
> four or five weeks close attendance, and continual rea-
> sonings with each other, our different sentiment on
> almost every question—several of the last producing
> as many noes as ays—is, methinks, a melancholy proof
> of the imperfection of the human understanding. We,
> indeed, seem to feel our own want of political wisdom,
> since we have been running about in search of it. We
> have gone back to ancient history for models of gov-
> ernment, and examined the different forms of those
> Republics which, having been formed with the seeds
> of their own dissolution, now no longer exist. And we
> have viewed modern States all round Europe, but find
> none of their Constitutions suitable to our circum-
> stances. In this situation of this Assembly, groping, as
> it were, in the dark to find political truth, and scarce
> able to distinguish it when presented to us, how has it
> happened, sir, that we have not hitherto once thought
> of humbly applying to the Father of Lights to illu-
> minate our understandings? In the beginning of the
> contest with Great Britain, when we were sensible of

danger, we had daily prayer in this room for divine protection. Our prayers, sir, were heard, and they were graciously answered. All of us who were engaged in the struggle must have observed frequent instances of a superintending Providence in our favor. To that kind Providence we owe this happy opportunity of consulting in peace on the means of establishing our future national felicity. And have we now forgotten that powerful friend? Or do we imagine that we no longer need His assistance.

I have lived, sir, a long time, and the longer I live the more convincing proofs I see of this truth—that God governs in the affairs of men; and if a sparrow cannot fall to the ground without His notice, is it probable that an empire can rise without His aid? We have been assured, sir, in the sacred writings, that "except the Lord build the house, they labor in vain that build it." I firmly believe this; and I also believe that without His concurring aid, we shall succeed in this political building no better than the builders of Babel. We shall be divided by our little partial local interests, our projects will be confounded, and we ourselves shall be become a reproach and a by-word down to future ages. And, what is worse, mankind may hereafter from this unfortunate instance, despair of establishing governments by human wisdom, and leave it to chance, war, and conquest.

I therefore beg leave to move, that henceforth prayers, imploring the assistance of Heaven, and its

blessings on our deliberations, be held in this assembly
every morning before we proceed to business, and that
one or more of the clergy of this city be requested to
officiate in that service.[3]

We may not be trying to establish a new country, but we
are fighting a reborn Leviathan. We need to resist the temptation to try to conform society to our will rather than to
reality; we need to work to restore those elements of our political philosophy drawn from the Christian tradition that
have been lost; we need to use all the tools at our disposal
to defend our rights and the rights of others. But we also
need to pray earnestly and deeply that Lincoln's words in the
Gettysburg Address would apply to us today: "that this nation, under God, shall have a new birth of freedom—and
that government of the people, by the people, for the people,
shall not perish from the earth." Amen.

3. Quoted by Lorenzo D. Johnson, *An Address to the Pastors and People of These United States on the Chaplaincy of the General Government Viewed in Its Connection with Extending the Redeemer's Name in the World* (Washington, D.C., 1857), 7.

SUGGESTIONS FOR FURTHER READING

Augustine, *The City of God*. Many editions available.

Brutus, Stephen Junius. *Vindiciae contra Tyrannos: A Defense of Liberty against Tyrants*. Translated by William Walker. Introduction by Glenn S. Sunshine. Canon Press, 2020.

Christianity and Freedom, Vol. I: Historical Perspectives. Edited by Timothy Samuel Shah and Allen D. Hertzke. Cambridge University Press, 2016.

Colson, Charles W. *God and Government: An Insider's View on the Boundaries between Faith and Politics*. Zondervan, 2007.

Ellazar, Daniel J. *The Covenant Tradition in Politics*, 3 volumes. Transaction Publishers, 1995–1998.

Grabill, Stephen J. *Recovering the Natural Law Tradition in Reformed Theological Ethics*. Eerdmans, 2006.

Guinness, Os. *A Free People's Suicide: Sustainable Freedom and the American Future*. IVP, 2013.

_____. *Last Call for Liberty: How America's Genius for Freedom Has become Its Greatest Threat*. IVP, 2018.

Hamilton, Alexander, et al. *The Federalist Papers*. Many editions available.

Höpfl, Harro (editor), *Luther and Calvin on Secular Authority*. Cambridge University Press, 1991.

Locke, John. *Two Treatises of Government and A Letter Concerning Toleration*. Many editions available.

Metaxas, Eric. *If You Can Keep It: The Forgotten Promise of American Liberty*. Penguin, 2017.

Novak, Michael. *Free Persons and the Common Good*. Madison Books, 1988.

_____. *On Two Wings: Humble Faith and Common Sense at America's Founding*. Encounter Books, 2001.

Rutherford, Samuel. *Lex Rex: The Law and the King*. Introduction by Douglas Wilson. Canon Press, 2020.

Stark, Rodney. *The Victory of Reason: How Christianity Led to Freedom, Capitalism, and Western Success*. Random House, 2006.

Tierney, Brian. *The Idea of Natural Rights*. Eerdmans, 1997.

Wetzel, James. *Augustine's City of God: A Critical Guide*. Cambridge University Press, 2014.

Witte, John. *Christianity and Human Rights: An Introduction*. Cambridge University Press, 2010.

_____. *Law and Protestantism: The Legal Teachings of the Lutheran Reformation*. Cambridge University Press, 2002.

_____. *The Reformation of Rights: Law, Religion and Human Rights in Early Modern Calvinism*. Cambridge University Press, 2008.

ACKNOWLEDGMENTS

This book began its life as two series of articles for the *World-view Journal*, a now defunct online publication of *BreakPoint* and the Colson Center for Christian Worldview. The articles focused on questions of the relationship of church and state and the circumstances in which Christians could engage in passive or active resistance to the government. I asked my daughter, Elizabeth Sunshine, an experienced writer and editor and a doctoral student in theology at Notre Dame, to help me edit the two series together. She did so, and that became the first draft of this book. I was not able to work on it right away due to multiple other writing projects, but I had a place to begin.

Then I joined with C.R. Wiley and Tom Price to start the *Theology Pugcast*, a podcast now carried on the Fight Laugh Feast Network. Once when it was my week to provide a topic, I opted to discuss Protestant resistance theory. That proved to be a remarkably popular episode, and so I decided the time was ripe to go back to the manuscript Elizabeth had prepared for me. There is a significant difference between the level of coverage needed in a book compared to articles, so everything needed to be expanded and new topics added, but from that base I then prepared the manuscript for the book.

Canon Press was quite interested in the project and gave me a great deal of leeway in outlining and developing the book. Not all publishers do that, and I want to acknowledge with thanks the freedom that Canon gave me in building the book around the themes I thought were important. Along with that, Brian Kohl, my editor at Canon, also made many valuable suggestions and recommendations that made this a better and more interesting book. Any deficiencies that remain are my own.